Jump Start *Your* Genealogy Research

Table of Contents

Introduction 9
Overview 13
Getting Started 21
    Organization 21
        Storage 21
        Binders 22
        Files 23
        Notes 23
        Forms 25
        Software 25
    Where to Start 25
Libraries and Archives 29
    Public and private libraries 29
    Periodical and Journals 32
        Periodical Source Index (PERSI) 33
        AGBI (American Genealogical Biographical Index) 33
    Historical and Genealogical Societies 34
    Newspapers 36
    Census 39
        Federal Population Census Questions: 41
        SLAVE SCHEDULES 45
    Maps 48
    History books 50
Military 53

Vintage Vickie Presents...

Jump Start *Your* Genealogy Research

Super Simple Steps

For Tracing Your Family Tree

By Vickie Chupurdia

Revised and updated - **30% more content!**

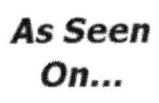

As Seen On... abc CBS NBC FOX

Revised from previous publication: 'The Book on Genealogy' 2012
Revised and updated 2014 – 30% more content

© Copyright by Vickie Chupurdia

Published By:
Autumn Leaf Publishing, 408 4th Avenue, Two Harbors, MN 55616

Printed in the United States of America. All rights reserved under International Copyright Law. Contents and/or cover may not be reproduced in whole or in part without express written consent of the publisher.

Disclaimer: Every effort has been made to accurately represent our product. We do not guarantee any individual will discover, find or locate any ancestral records or persons

    Military in general 53

    Pensions 54

    Land and Bounty Claims 60

    Organizations 60

    Gravesites 61

    Medical Records 63

Court Houses 65

    Vital Statistics 65

    Adoption Records 67

    Death Records 68

    Marriage Records 69

    Divorce Records 70

    Immigration or Emigration 70

        What's the difference? *70*

    Ship Records 73

    Court 75

    Land / Deed Records 76

    Taxes 78

Around Town 81

    Employment Records 81

    Churches 82

    Cemeteries 82

    Schools 86

    City Directories 87

    Prisons/ Hospitals / Institutions 87

    Museums 88

    Reenactments 89

    Culture 90

Technology 93
   Where to begin? 93
   Resources Online 97
Citations/Questionnaires/Forms 107
   Citations 107
   Questionnaires and Interviews 113
   Forms and Charts 114
Genetics and DNA 117
   What is DNA? 117
   DNA Testing 118
Sharing Your Family History 121
   Use Your Imagination 121
   Kissing Cousins 123
Summary 125
Appendix 129
   Questionnaire for Interviewing 129
About the Author – Vintage Vickie 135

What do our memories do if they aren't being shared?

What do our stories do if they're not being told?

They fade with time and are forgotten.

www.VintageVickie.com.

Introduction

Hi! I'm Vickie Chupurdia, 'Your Genealogy Success Coach', also known as 'Vintage Vickie'. I'm going to share with you some insider secrets to getting started digging up your roots. Use these tips and you're on your way to becoming a great genealogist.

I started doing genealogy research over 30 years ago. Back then I had no computer and no internet. There were no online data bases or history sites with search options. I had three young children and lived in a very small mining town in northeastern Minnesota, which was conveniently located in the middle of nowhere.

This made genealogy research very cumbersome. I wrote many, many letters to court houses and waited weeks for replies. Then I would have to send in the fee for copies of the records and wait weeks for the results to come in the mail. I drove over 60 miles one way to the nearest library of any size. There I would order micro-fiche or books through the inter library loan system and again, wait weeks for them to arrive.

I would have to research in the library to find out even WHERE to write. I needed addresses of court houses, libraries, historical societies, genealogy societies and a variety of other sources.

Don't misunderstand me. You will still need to use libraries, court houses, museums and more. They are treasure houses. They are chock full of information. They are a genealogist's haven. But, I will show you how to be prepared to get the most 'bang' for your time.

My parents lived in the same town that I did and every time a relative came to visit I cornered them and picked their brains for family history and clues for further research.

At every family reunion while the young adults my age were visiting and having a beer I was sitting with all of the people in their senior years asking questions. But, I preferred it that way. It fascinated me. I loved hearing their stories and they loved telling them.

I had no laptop so I became very adept at taking notes quickly. Occasionally I was able to record someone in a one on one session but most of the time there was a room full of people and the recorder's microphone wouldn't pick up all of the conversation.

Times have sure changed. Now I can get an address to a court house or library in seconds on the internet. I can find out their hours of operation, policies, fees and more in just minutes. I can even get a map with directions to their exact location.

But as valuable as the internet is, it does not have all of the answers. More and more data bases are being made available on the internet all of the time; but there comes a time when you have to go beyond Google.

This book will help you find clues and answers. A secret treasure is just waiting to be dug up by you. Happy digging!

Overview

Just what is the difference between genealogy, family tree research and being a historian?

Genealogy is the factual account of the descent of a person, or their family or ancestor. It is the proof of the lineage that follows the lines from son to parent, to grandparent, to great grandparent, and so on.

Family Tree Research is more or less a synonym for genealogy research. The family tree itself is the charting of the lineage lines.

Personal Historian is someone that compiles the memoirs or stories in some form. This can be a simple one topic report, a full book, audio or video recordings, CD's, DVD's and more. A Personal Historian doesn't usually delve deeply into the genealogy aspect. They may help briefly with the research but their main concern is to preserve the stories.

Overview

Family Historian is an expansion of the facts. To be a family historian you not only chart the lineage but you research the background, location, local history, world history, family stories, lifestyles, politics and more.

You add substance to the facts. You discover the why's and how's. Recreating the time your ancestor lived you infuse that information through narrative into your research.

Most of us are interested in all aspects of these definitions. I know I'm thrilled when I find another name to add to my tree. As soon as the name is put in print I start to wonder about that person and what kind of life they lived.

The family historian in me goes to work to fill in all of the blanks. Both are satisfying, but to me the family historian is by far the most interesting part of doing the research.

If you're just beginning your historical quest it may seem like a daunting task before you. Relax, coming up I'll give you some great tips to help get you started.

To be a successful genealogist you need to realize that you will be continually learning about new sources and methods for research. There is no one out there that knows everything. All of us learn as we go because each ancestor's search is unique. There are generalities for all of them but your quest will steer you in a special direction for every one of your family members.

For example did you know that there is a 'Transcriptions of Gravestones of Servicemen' from various wars in our

Jump Start Your Genealogy Research

Nation's history? There are military rosters and muster rolls.

For example the Daughters of the American Revolution have books listing Revolutionary War soldiers. Each state might have books of just their own soldiers. Much of this information was recently made available online at www.dar.org.

There are more records at a court house than just birth and death records. There are land records, tax records, Wills and plat maps.

Churches have more than cemeteries next to them. They have birth, baptismal, marriage, and death records. Some of them have photo histories where you might find your relative. Some of you may have even posed for pictures yourself for the church registry. The church history may indicate that your relative was a Sunday School Teacher in 1910.

You might find some obscure little county history book put together by the local citizens in a tiny little public library in the middle of nowhere only to find out that 3 full pages deal entirely with your ancestors. This happened to me in Wheeling, MO.

The chances of this type of small publication are slim to make it into the huge databases that are online. You have to go to the source or find someone local to do it for you.

So like I said, you will be continually learning about new resources. While looking for one thing a helpful librarian might say, "Oh, if you like this information you might try the 'so and so' history center in Chillicothe.

Overview

They have taken over most of the county historical items and they have an extensive research library." So, on your way you go.

With that in mind, you will encounter many, many experts along the way but there is no way any one 'expert' has all of the answers. The woman you meet at the Germanna History Center in Virginia may fill your notebook with facts about those early settlers. However, she may know nothing about the first German settlers in Milwaukee, Wisconsin.

I can't stress enough to be polite to all of these librarians and research assistants. They are busy people. Please appreciate the time they spend helping you. Make sure you get their name. I often send thank you notes after I have visited their library or center. It helps in case you need them to send you additional copies of something or do more research in your absence; they are much more willing to help out.

I'd like to give you a word of warning. As a new genealogist you might get excited to find out that someone has posted your entire family tree out on the internet. All of the research has been completed by someone else. Don't believe it. There are many people who don't know what they are doing and they are dumping bad genealogies onto the web. Others are grabbing them and accepting them as true. Make sure everything is accurate. Check to see if they have citations to back up their facts.

I'm not saying all genealogies on the internet are bad but I have run across more than I can count that were inaccurate. Sometimes they have the mother only 8 years older than the daughter. They found a person on the 1870 census that matched the name of their ancestor and claimed it as their own without checking it further- only to find out that person died before their son was born and it was just a coincidence that they had the same name.

Posted family trees are great sources for clues. If you are able to contact the poster ask them for their proof and citations. If they have none then you MUST get your own proof. Use the clues and find out if what they say is accurate. I'm sorry to tell you that many times it isn't.

Also, don't believe those companies that will send you your family crest or 'Coat of Arms' for a fee. Most people did not have a family crest and this is often a scam. The crest is a part of the entire 'Coat of Arms'. In England, direct descent is required for any heir to have the legal right to bear his ancestor's coat of arms.

In an article written by Kimberly Powell she says, "Except for a few individual exceptions from some parts of Eastern Europe, there is no such thing as a coat of arms for a surname or family name. Coats of arms belong to individuals, not families or surnames. For a person to have a right to a coat of arms, they must have either had it granted to them or be descended in the legitimate male line from the person to whom the coat of arms was originally granted.

How could a company that has not researched your family tree know whether you have inherited the right to display a particular coat of arms? If you're looking for something fun then these gifts are OK, though misrepresentative, but if you're looking for something

Overview

from your own family history, then stay away!" http://genealogy.about.com/od/basics/ss/scams_5.htm

Don't share your information too easily. You might be contacted by someone claiming to be your 3rd cousin and they want to swap information. You fire off your entire file and receive nothing in return. You have just provided that person with full names, date and location of birth and relationship that could assist in identity theft. Remember, secret passwords or security questions you set up on many of your online accounts are your mother's maiden name and now they have it.

If you ever feel like you want to upload all of your information onto the Web please don't upload any information pertaining to living individuals. You are violating their privacy rights.

What kind of genealogist do you want to be? Do you want to collect every scrap of information you can about any relative, even your third cousin once removed? Or do you want to stick to direct line lineage research and only branch out occasionally to look for clues that might assist you in your research?

In studying direct line lineage you inevitably have to expand to siblings, cousins, neighborhoods, church memberships and so on. You will gather valuable insight and information about your family. A sibling's obituary or Will may provide you with valuable information. People often emigrated together and you may find clues to discovering your female ancestor's maiden name by studying who traveled with them. However, you don't have to have them in your database if you don't want to. You only need to use the information as a source citation to prove something for your direct line.

Genealogy is basically one big jigsaw puzzle. You have to be a super sleuth detective. You search for clues and like a Nancy Drew mystery each clue leads you to another. You piece together the clues into a wonderful historical story of your family.

In order to keep track of your clues you should use genealogy charts and family group sheets to record all of the information that you gather. There are websites that offer free downloadable charts to get you started. There are many software programs that will assist you in tracking your data but you don't need software. You can start out just like I did with the old-fashioned paper records.

Starting out with a paper system also helps you understand the entire process for charts, numbering systems and record keeping. You can always transfer your information to a software program at a later date. You get a chance to see if you like family tree research without investing very much money.

It's important to keep track of your research, even when you don't find the answer you were looking for. If you record when and where you have looked you won't waste time looking there again.

This could be something as simple as a notebook with the date, place and documents you reviewed. You can have dividers by surname, state, or whatever works for you. You need to record the date, the location of the source, the description of the source such as title,

Overview

author, newspaper, (date, column and paragraph), and some notes explaining what you found.

Family Tree Research is wonderfully rewarding. Family legends of love/hate, war, hardships, marriage, joy, adventure, and more are just waiting to be uncovered by you. Enjoy your research. Don't make it work or drudgery. Have fun

Getting Started

Organization

Organization is a key ingredient in being a successful genealogist. You absolutely must keep accurate records and know where to find those records. Your research isn't valid unless you have accurate proof and documentation of that proof. There are a variety of ways to accomplish this depending on how much data and memorabilia you have.

Storage

Where will you store important family memorabilia and documents? A dark damp basement is not the place. Make sure they are protected. There are many storage methods you can use depending on your budget. It can be anything from large plastic tubs for some items to acid free paper between photographs.

Perhaps you're more like me and like the idea of displaying your historical treasures by hanging photographs and documents on the wall. I am lucky to have in my possession some very old and large charcoal drawings of my great and great-great grandparents. I feel a strong connection to them as I pass by them throughout the day. Just a glance often makes me wonder what they would have been doing in their lives. What chores would they be doing? How would they be spending their evenings?

Binders

For those of you starting out with the paper method, start a three ring binder for each major branch of your family tree. Label them with the surname. This is where you will keep Family Group Sheets and Charts. Three ring binders are better than spiral notebooks. You have the capability to rearrange, insert or remove information easily. You can purchase inexpensive dividers to separate the sections. You might want sections for bible records, cemetery, census, correspondence, and so on.

You can also keep a master binder that has the pedigree charts, and notes on where your other data is located and how it is filed.

If you are researching a certain geographical area to learn more about the type of lives your family led you could have a binder for each state or area such as Virginia or Original Colonies.

Later when you decide to write your family history you will incorporate this information to explain the day to day living of your family. Family history is more than just Susie's parents were John and Mary. We want to know where they lived, what jobs they held, was there war at the time, who was president, and so on.

One of the most important things that any successful genealogist will advise you on is to get organized from the start. Don't put it off thinking, "I'll put this in some sort of order later". Later never comes and before you know it you have a mountain of paper scraps tucked here and there.

Files

You can't keep everything in a 3 ring binder. Develop a filing system early. You should have a place designated for all documents. You want to be able to retrieve your information when you need it. Whether it's legal documentation, pamphlets, and brochures or your notes from the last family reunion, everything should be filed in a system that makes sense to you.

You may want to purchase a filing cabinet or at least filing tubs. There are plastic tubs that are made specifically for hanging file folders. It also makes it easy to take with you on a field trip.

Files could mirror the same labeling system you developed for your 3 ring binders and dividers. You may also want to make a file just for library brochures which state hours and directions, or a file for planned research ideas.

Notes

I can't stress enough to take accurate notes. Whether you are interviewing a family member or researching in a library. Often you don't get back to your paperwork for

Getting Started

weeks after the initial trip to the library and your notes suddenly don't make sense to you.

Carry a notebook with you at all times. You never know when a family member or a magazine article you're reading at the doctor's office will trigger a thought or a need to write something down.

When Great Grandmother Sarah starts reminiscing, you need to be prepared. You might forget the details of her story and you may never get the opportunity to have her repeat it in quite the same way or with the same emotion.

Something you saw on the History Channel on T.V. could provide a clue triggering an idea for new research. You might be on a trip and find yourself passing a small local history museum. The museum could hold artifacts and documents to help you in your search.

You might be reading a book on the plane and it mentions a location where you know your family lived. It might describe the town or other prominent residents at the time.

I have been known to write on napkins, the backs of bank deposits or anything else I could find because I didn't have my valuable notebook with me at the time.

Don't forget to transcribe or at least make a copy of the pages in your notebook on regular intervals. Your heart will sink if you find out that you accidentally left a notebook full of information at the restaurant and when you went back to get it they threw it out.

Forms

There are many websites that offer free downloadable forms such as Questionnaires, Pedigree Charts, Family Group sheets, and so on. Make copies of all of these forms and have blanks handy in your filing system. One source is: http://www.genealogysearch.org/free/forms.html

Software

There are many choices for the genealogist when it comes to software. The top software choices are easy to use, come with tutorials, and the top 3 are under $30.00. You can get a review by the experts of the top ten software choices at http://genealogy-software-review.toptenreviews.com. It sure beats the paper trail I used years ago. They are well worth the money.

Always, always back up your work. I save to an external drive in case my computer crashes. I also periodically make CD's and give to another family member for safe keeping.

Where to Start

The first and most important rules of genealogy are to start with yourself and work backwards. You might want to just jump into great grandmother's story from the late 1800's but you will do yourself a great favor if you approach it more systematically.

Take the time to start with yourself and work backwards. You might find out information that will enlighten your search of great grandma. You may miss that your grandmother was born in another state and later they

Getting Started

showed up on a census in yet a different location. Why did they move? What is their story? If you don't do it step by step you may miss important clues.

Fill out a pedigree chart and family group sheet about yourself. Don't worry about the gaps now; you will fill that in as you get the information. Gather your records. Get copies of your birth certificate, baptism, marriage or divorce, school records or diploma, military records, and so on. Your children and other family members will love you for it in years to come. Do you have photographs of you all through school, or of your wedding?

Just a side note here... Please, please write on the back of each and every photograph the names of the people, place and date. 50 years from now somebody might be trying to go through your photographs and nobody will have a clue as to who the people are. Don't write on the back something like 'this is me and my cousin Mike'. Who is 'me'? Will they know 50 years from now?

Today many of us store our photos on our computers. The same applies. Please write 'captions' or file names for each and every photo. Back them up to a CD. It will be so helpful years from now.

Next, move on to your parents and record their information in the same manner. Look on the back of photos to see if you can get any clues to steer your research. Do they have scrap books with newspaper clippings? Remember to treat these items carefully. Old photos and scrapbooks are their treasures and the sentimental value is high. It just keeps growing from there. You will be surprised how quickly your tree expands.

Jump Start Your Genealogy Research

You and your spouse are two. Add both of your parents and you have 4 more. Continue on with their parents (your grandparents) and now you have 8 more; another generation and its 16 more. That's already 30 people. This is just the direct line; child to parent. Fill in the leaves of the branches by adding all of the siblings for each generation and you not only have a tree you have the makings of a forest!

As you concentrate on each line find out as much as possible about brothers and sisters or cousins. Many genealogists don't realize how important this is. You may lose track of someone in your direct line. Perhaps they moved and were missed on a census record. Perhaps they never owned their own land. Whatever the reason you may have trouble finding them. Keeping accurate records of siblings and other relatives may give you excellent clues as to where they ended up. Maybe you find them mentioned on one of the siblings wills.

Now that you have the basics from gathering what your family has to offer it's time to branch out. Therefore, you have to decide which branch of your tree you want to tackle. It is perfectly okay to work on more than one branch at a time. However, try to do too much at once and the names and places start mixing all together and nothing makes sense. Start with one surname and work with it for awhile then go on to the next.

Remember it isn't just who gave birth to who. It's about the geography and history of the area. It's about the politics and inventions of the time. You may have to study American history or historical maps to see the boundaries of a county or state during that time period. You want to be able to 'walk' in your ancestor's shoes.

Getting Started

Track your progress and your research, even the book where you found nothing. Don't duplicate your search in the future.

Libraries and Archives

Public and private libraries

When it's time to expand your research there are many types of public and private libraries, archives, family history centers, historical societies, genealogical societies, ethnic societies and more for you to visit.

Before you head off to any of these places you need to do a different kind of research. You need to contact them and find out their hours, days of operation and any rules or regulations they may have.

If the library is not located in your immediate area you can look them up on the internet. Many of them will have their hours of operation and location listed on the site. I would still call ahead just to make sure there isn't some special holiday or special interest group that will be there that day. The library staff is already very busy and you don't want to show up on the same day that the 8th grade class is having a field trip to study local

Libraries and Archives

history. They may also have a map or directions on their web site.

If the library doesn't have its own web site, visit the Chamber of Commerce web site or call them. They will have the contact information about the libraries in that area.

Questions to ask the library:

1. Do you have a genealogy section?
2. Do you have a local history section?
3. Do you allow photo copies? What is the cost? Many will not allow you to do the photo copying but will do it for you.
4. What tools may I bring? Many libraries will only allow pencils, not pens or computers.
5. Do you allow computer laptops and/or scanners? (If they do it would only be flatbed scanners not the 'feed' scanners.)
6. Directions
7. Is there parking available? Is there a fee?
8. Do they have records on microfilm?
9. What types of records do they have? (Newspapers, census records, county books, city directories, etc.)
10. Do I need a photo ID?
11. Do they allow digital cameras?
12. Some will not allow backpacks, purses or any kind of bags.
13. Some will not allow jackets or anything with pockets. They don't want any of their artifacts disappearing.
14. Do they have small lockers for rent to put your belongings in?

15. Are there any other fees?
16. If it's a private society is it open to the public or do you need an appointment?

Next, I repeat, get organized. What is your goal? Is this a long trip for you? Do you want to be able to visit the court house in this city during the same trip? Maybe you should go to the library on a Saturday and the court house during its open hours Monday through Friday. Do you need reservations at a hotel? How long will it take you to get there? What will the costs be in gas, lodging and meals?

Write out an outline of your goals and what you hope to achieve during the library visit. Do you want to concentrate on local histories since you can check census records online? Do you want to look at historical maps or local newspapers? Are you looking for a particular surname? Decide which files or 3 ring notebooks you need to bring. Pack extra pencils, blank forms, a magnifying glass, and rolls of quarters if you are using a copy machine or small bills to pay for photocopying.

There are many large and well known libraries for genealogy research such as the Allen County, Indiana public library. Take advantage of any orientation tours they offer. It will save you a lot of time in your quest.

Don't forget the tiny little library in the town of 200 people. I found a treasure in family history in such a place in their county history book. Beware though, this is a secondary source. You must validate any of the information provided.

Libraries and Archives

Periodical and Journals

Check periodicals, also known as newsletters, magazines and quarterlies. There are many periodicals that have been around for years and they are available for you to review.

Although genealogical periodicals offer many sources of hidden information, they are often overlooked by genealogists in searching for family history.

Indexes or extracts of every type of record imaginable are available, such as cemetery inscriptions, baptisms, naturalization records, and homestead applications. Periodicals are usually published by local genealogical societies and list family names and history of particular regions.

Most periodicals have annual cumulative indexes that make it possible to review a year's listings at one time. But even more helpful are the indexes that bring together information from several periodicals combine the listings for several years. Some of them index information by subject, locality, and personal name in addition to family name.

Journals, such as The American Genealogist (TAG) and the New England Historical & Genealogical Register focus on publishing compiled genealogies of families. The National Genealogy Quarterly focuses on case studies and learning good research skills.

A couple of older periodicals are The New England Genealogical Society, or the Maryland Historical Magazine that goes back to the 1930's. There are so many that I couldn't begin to list them here. Many states have their own.

Newer publications are magazines like The Heritage Quest, Family Chronicle and Genealogy Helper.

Periodical Source Index (PERSI)

Periodical Source Index (PERSI) is a multi-volume set published by the Allen County Public Library in Fort Wayne, Indiana. www.acpl.lib.in.us.

Created by the staff of the Historical Genealogy Department, PERSI is the largest subject index to genealogical and historical periodical articles in the world. Many of these records cannot be found online.

AGBI (American Genealogical Biographical Index)

The American Genealogical-Biographical Index (AGBI) is an awesome genealogical collection and is equal to over 200 printed volumes in one database.

2 million or more individual name references are listed that appeared in the Boston Transcript from over 40 years of publication. Most of this material has never been published anywhere else.

The AGBI database contains millions of records of the people whose names have appeared in printed genealogical records and family histories. Some large libraries have copies of this information or it can be viewed online at Ancestry's American Genealogical-Biographical Index. When on Ancestry search the card catalog and enter AGBI and the search results will display. Click on the Index name and enter your search criteria.

Remember this is an index. The actual record may be housed somewhere else. Most of the works referenced in the AGBI are housed at the Godfrey Memorial Library in Connecticut. A photocopy service is available. Please contact Godfrey Memorial Library at 134 Newfield St, Middletown, CT 06457 or via e-mail at referenceinfo@godfrey.org to make use of this service.

Of course, you may already know that the largest genealogical collection in the world is through the Church of Jesus Christ of Latter Day Saints (Mormons). The main library is located in Salt Lake City, Utah but they have thousands of branch libraries in several countries. They also do inter-library loans and many of their records are available online.

Historical and Genealogical Societies

Historical and Genealogical Societies often have wonderful collections and research opportunities for the genealogist. Some are quite large like the Minnesota Historical Society which is responsible for several historical libraries, sites and museums. Most of the smaller societies are run by volunteers and their hours of operation vary greatly. Some are only open by appointment, some only on weekends, and some only in the summer and so on. Call ahead. Many of these volunteers are passionate about family history and are pleased to help you.

The National Archives in Washington, DC has a huge collection of primary source documents including census records, Wills, military records, land records, and more. There are also many state and county archives. Archives differ from libraries in that instead of books, microfilm and publications the archives will have the original source documents for the history to that region. They have many branches throughout the United States.

Some libraries do offer research services by mail for a fee but most are under staffed. They may occasionally answer requests but please remember to ask only one or two questions. Don't ask them to send you everything on your great uncle John Johnson.

Include the information they need to do the search. They don't need to know your entire history. Try to keep the questions simple and direct. Write surnames in all capitals. Include alternate name spellings, nicknames or any other quirks that they may encounter doing the search.

Include telephone numbers, e-mails and your address so they may contact you if they have questions. Enclose a self-addressed stamped envelope and the agreed upon fee for the research. Also, please send a thank you note. Many of these librarians are going out of their way to help you. Keep a copy of the letter for your records.

Call ahead and ask:

1. Do they offer research services?
2. What is the fee? (Even if they don't have a fee it is always nice to include a few dollars to cover the photocopying expenses.)
3. What is the response time?
4. Any other regulations they may have.

Libraries and Archives

Newspapers

You can step into the past reviewing old newspapers. The advertisements show you the fashions of the time period and the costs for goods. What people were most likely to be buying and various types of stores, businesses and services provided.

Newspapers had gossip columns or the social page, birth, death and marriage notices, editorials, legal notices and of course the obituaries and the actual news of the time.

There are several online resources for viewing old newspapers records. The online resources have come a long way in recent years but there are many, many newspapers that have yet to find their way to the internet. Try www.newspapers.com or www.genealogybank.com.

Many of the libraries, historical societies or archives will have the local newspapers on microfilm. The larger state libraries and societies may have copies of several of the smaller newspapers as well as the big city papers.

Remember that many newspapers are biased in their editorials and political views. Two newspapers in the same town may battle against each other and have completely different stories about the same event.

Let's look at some of the things included in the newspaper. We'll start with the most obvious for the researcher and that's the obituaries and deaths.

From the obituary you will probably find out date and place of birth, names of siblings, and other relatives.

Jump Start Your Genealogy Research

You may find out their occupation, or military service. You will be able to find out their religious affiliation from the name of the church where the services were held. The obituary may list the name of the cemetery where they were buried.

You might find out any organizations they belonged to such as the VFW or local art club. Obituaries are printed sometimes weeks after the death. Either the family didn't submit it to the paper or the paper is only printed weekly or monthly.

Birth announcements or baptisms may also be found in newspapers. It will list the parents and often the grandparents or other relatives. The name of the church, date of the birth and so on.

Wedding announcements or anniversary announcements appear in the local news. Sometimes they tell the parents of the bride and groom or the children of those celebrating their anniversary. Anniversary announcements may give a detailed history of the couple and their lives together.

The legal section may also report any marriage applications. A news worthy article may be a report of the wedding itself and tell you about the ceremony, what the bride wore, the bridesmaids and groomsmen.

Society sections in the smaller newspapers are quite fun to read. It may say that Mary Nay journeyed to Chicago by train to visit her niece Phoebe Martin. Or the local Elks Club elected new officers and lists them by name. Society pages may also be where you find church announcements.

Libraries and Archives

Classified sections and other announcements might tell you of someone owing debts, or offering services, and estate sales.

Legal sections tell about Wills and estates, land sales or other real estate transactions, taxes, divorces, and more. Delinquent taxes might have been printed in the local newspapers so remember to check that section.

During war time there may be a section devoted to the military and the news about the local men and women in the service. It may list visits home, transfers, where they are fighting, or deaths.

Schools and other local organizations may print notices of someone winning an award, school board minutes or elections and of course graduations. The sports column may tell you that your grandfather was a great football player.

Announcements of the county fair and who or what will be there and other attractions coming to town may be included in the newspaper. Did your great-grandmother win a blue ribbon for the best apple pie in the county? Did Uncle Bob have the best draft horses? Did Steve win the calf roping contest? Was your aunt a winner of the 'Miss Peach Cobbler' beauty contest?

Local elections for city council, county sheriff or other offices and their campaigns might be found in the newspaper. Elections are in the fall so look during that time period or prior for election campaign articles.

There are other types of newspapers such as a local shopper or a church/organization newsletter.

Don't forget the photographs! You might find a photo of your uncle when he was elected to the city council, a photograph of Main Street or the retail store your grandfather owned. A photo of great-grandma winning that pie contest I mentioned above.

Unfortunately, there are many mistakes and inaccuracies in newspapers; misprints or inverted dates or the wrong spelling of a name. Newspapers offer valuable information but please try to verify the data with other documents if possible.

Census

Although you can find census records online many libraries have them on microfilm. Federal census records are the life blood of genealogists. Records are confidential for 72 years, by law. The 1940 records were recently released for public use in 2012.

Depending on the year, different censuses asked different questions (see below). Census records started in the United States in 1790 and were conducted every 10 years after that. 1850 and 1860 included slave schedules. 1890 census was destroyed by a fire in the national Archives in 1921. Only a few thousand names were salvaged. 1940 is the latest census currently available.

Realize that there are other census records. There are state and local census records too. Some American colonies took censuses before the federal government did and some territories conducted their own censuses. Since federal censuses were conducted every ten years

Libraries and Archives

the state or local censuses might fill in gaps for the years in between.

State censuses asked different questions than the federal census. Not all states took a census but most, took them every 10 years on the five year mark; (1895) whereas; the federal census is on the zero mark (1900). State records can usually be found at the state archives or library.

When searching the census look for 'homes' or 'institutions' for the aged, orphans, insane, retired military and so on.

There are other types of census records besides the Population Censuses. These include Agriculture, Industry, Manufacturing and Social Statistics censuses. Your ancestor may have been missed on the Population Census but you find him reporting how many beans he grew on the Agricultural Census.

Some of the things you can learn from Population Census records:

1. Names of all of those in the household. This may include a servant, boarder or elderly parent that may give you the clue to your female's maiden name.
2. Ages of all in the household
3. years married
4. Place of birth cx
5. If they can read or write
6. Color of hair or eyes.
7. Neighbors or other relatives nearby
8. Country of origin
9. And more...

Federal Population Census Questions:

The following is a list of the column headings and questions asked on each census.

1790

Name of family head; free white males of 16 years and up; free white males under 16; free white females; slaves; other free persons.

1800

Names of family head; if white, age and sex; race; slaves.

1810

Name of family head; if white, age and sex; race; slaves.

1820

Name of family head; age; sex; race; foreign-ers not naturalized; slaves; industry (agriculture, commerce, and manufactures).

1830

Name of family head; age; sex; race; foreign-ers not naturalized; slaves; industry.

1840

Name of family head; age; sex; race; slaves; num-ber of deaf and dumb; number of blind; number of insane and idiotic and whether in public or private charge; number of persons in each family employed in each of six classes of industry and one of occupation; literacy; pensioners for Revolu¬tionary or military service.

1850

Name; age; sex; race; whether deaf and dumb, blind, insane, or idiotic; value of real estate; occupation; birthplace; whether married within the year; school attendance; literacy; whether a pauper or convict.

Supplemental schedules for slaves, and persons who died during the year.

1860

Name; age; sex; race; value of real estate; value of personal estate; occupation; birthplace; whether married within the year; school attendance; literacy; whether deaf and dumb; blind, insane, idiotic, pauper, or convict.

Supplemental schedules for slaves, and persons who died during the year.

1870

Name; age; race; occupation; value of real estate; value of personal estate; birthplace; whether parents were foreign born; month of birth if born within the year; month of marriage if married within the year; school attendance; literacy; whether deaf and dumb, blind, insane, or idiotic; male citizens 21 and over, and number of such persons denied the right to vote for other than rebellion. Supplemental schedule for persons who died during the year.

1880

Address; name, relationship to family head; sex; race; age; marital status; month of birth if born within the census year; occupation; months unemployed during the year; sickness or temporary disability; whether blind, deaf and dumb, idiotic, insane, maimed, crippled, bedridden, or otherwise disabled; school attendance; literacy; birthplace of person and parents. Supplemental schedules for persons who died during the year.

1890

General schedules--destroyed. Supplemental schedules for Union veterans of the Civil War and their widows.

1900

Address; name; relationship to family head; sex; race; age; marital status; number of years married; for women, number of children born and number now living; birthplace of person and parents; if foreign born, year of immigration and whether naturalized; occupation; months not employed; school attendance; literacy; ability to speak English; whether on a farm; home owned or rented and if owned, whether mortgaged.

1910

Address; name; relationship to family head; sex; race; age; marital status; number of years of present marriage for women, number of children born and number now living; birthplace and mother tongue of person and parents; if foreign born, year of immigration, whether naturalized, and whether able to speak English, or if not, language spoken; occupation, industry, and class of worker; if an employee, whether out of work during year; literacy; school attendance; home owned or rented; if owned, whether mortgaged; whether farm or house; whether a survivor of Union or Confederate Army or Navy; whether blind or deaf and dumb.

1920

Address; name; relationship to family head; sex; race; age; marital status; if foreign born, year of immigration to the U.S., whether naturalized, and year of naturalization; school attendance; literacy; birthplace of person and parents; mother tongue of foreign born; ability to speak English; occupation, industry, and class of worker; home owned or rented; if owned, whether free or mortgaged.

1930

Address; name; relationship to family head; home owned or rented; value or monthly rental; radio set; whether on a farm; sex; race; age; marital status; age at first marriage; school attendance; literacy; birthplace of person and parents; if foreign-born language spoken in home before coming to U.S., year of immigration, whether naturalized, and ability to speak English; occupation, industry, and class of worker; whether at work previous day (or last regular working day); veteran status; for Indians, whether of full or mixed blood, and tribal affiliation.

1940

Address; home owned or rented; value or monthly rental; whether on a farm; name; relationship to household head; sex; race; age; marital status; school attendance; educational attainment; birthplace; citizenship of foreign born; location of residence 5 years ago and whether on a farm; employment status; if at work, whether in private or nonemergency government work, or in public emergency work (WPA, CCC, NYA, etc.); if in private work, hours worked in week; if seeking work or on public emergency work, duration of unemployment; occupation, industry, and class of worker; weeks worked last year, income last year.

SLAVE SCHEDULES

It is difficult but not entirely impossible to trace ancestors that may have been enslaved. In 1870 the government had the first population census that gave the former slave by name. Checking similar surnames for others in the census may give clues as to who the owner was.

The Slave schedules were added to the federal census in 1850 and 1860. However, names of the individual slaves weren't listed; only the names of the owners.

1850 was also the first years that every member of every household was to be counted. That means it was also the first year for women and children, as well as slaves.

Included on the census was: Names of the Slave owners; number of slaves; age, sex, color of the slave; Fugitives from the state (did the slave flee and not return);

Libraries and Archives

number manumitted (released from slavery); Deaf & Dumb, blind, insane or idiotic.

It isn't much to go on most of the time. However, some of the schedules did list the names. If they were over 100 years old they may have even gotten a paragraph or more written about them. The census can be used to support other documentation and proof you may have.

Records for slave holdings can be found in other places besides the government census records. If you suspect you know the name of the owner you will need to research the owner.

In addition to census records try looking at other resources. Slave names may have been listed on purchase/sale documents, tax records, deeds transferred, wills, marriage records, Bible records, church and cemetery records and the owner's business records. Try to find historical recordings and writings of former slaves as they may provide valuable clues.

Check state, county and local government records, historical societies and genealogical societies for data, documents and photographs they may have.

If you are lucky enough to trace your slave ancestry back to the 1870 census you may be able to use the information and proof to verify your ancestor on the Slave schedules.

The slave schedule was used in the following states: Alabama, Arkansas, Delaware, Florida, Georgia, Kentucky, Louisiana, Maryland, Mississippi, Missouri, New Jersey, North Carolina, South Carolina, Tennessee, Texas and Virginia.

Jump Start Your Genealogy Research

A great web site to go to is: www.Myslaveancestors.com. There are several more. Just enter Slave Schedules in the search engine and you will receive several sites.

For many years during the American colonial period the white servants were much more numerous than the blacks. Many were indentured servitude, meaning someone paid their passage or provided room and board for them in exchange for servitude for a determined number of years - 7, 14, 20, it varied. This was equal to slavery in all points except the blacks were slaves for eternity.

Use the Soundex system and look at various spellings of a name. Soundex is a phonetic algorithm for indexing names by sound. Often the census taker may have been an immigrant themselves and spelled according to their knowledge. Handwriting is difficult to transcribe and records were damaged. Using the Soundex system helps you determine if there are other possible ways to spell or 'sound' your name. Don't forget nicknames.

To use the census Soundex system you need to know the person's name and the state/territory where they lived at the time of the census. If you know the name of the head of the household listed that will help. You might be able to find the person you are looking for listed under them.

Every Soundex code consists of a letter and 3 numbers. The letter is the first letter of the surname and the remaining letters are represented by numbers.

Rootsweb has a great Soundex converter: http://resources.rootsweb.ancestry.com/cgi-bin/soundexconverter

Libraries and Archives

I found ancestors with my last name, Chupurdia under Chupurdija, Cupurdija, Cupordia, and more. One of my ancestors, Eleanor can be found as Ellenor, Elenor, Elenore, and Eleanore.

If you know where they lived but can't find them you may have to resort to scrolling through the pages of the location. I always do this anyway. I look at several pages before and after my ancestor to see who their neighbors were. Often they were relatives, maybe the female's parents. Census takers went from house to house, or farm to farm in the same neighborhoods.

If you can't find them by their last name and they have an unusual first name try searching the census index by just the first name. (Soundex searches are by surname.)

Maps

Purchase a good atlas. The USA atlases come large enough to have a lot of detail but not so big that you can't bring them with you on a research trip. You know the kind I'm talking about, the Rand McNally Road Atlas types. These are good starting points.

If you are concentrating on a particular state you might want to purchase a folded map of that state. You can get these at book stores or if you live in that state at a local service station or even Walmart.

Also readily available are atlases or gazetteers of detailed topographical areas. For example, I have a gazetteer that that shows all of the rivers, forestry roads, state forests, elevations, county lines and more.

Jump Start Your Genealogy Research

You are going to find legal descriptions of the land. This is where a plat maps comes in handy. You know what I mean - the NW ¼ of the NE ¼ of Section 12, T10N, R8W, 160 acres. The easiest thing to do is start from the end and word backwards. The description is 160 acres that are in Range 8 West, which is in Township 10 North, which is in Section 12. Section 12 is divided into fourths. Locate the NE quarter and from that quarter find the NW quarter. There is your land. It is much easier to see on a land map and the staff will assist you. Once you see it in picture or map form it makes much more sense.

Plat maps are usually found at the court house but many libraries and historical societies also house them. Plat maps contain maps of acreage, parcels, boundaries and landownership. They may include public and private roadways, waterways, railways, municipal boundaries, school districts, political boundaries and more. Libraries or courthouses may have plat maps from many years prior showing land ownership.

You can also develop your own maps indicating the migrations route of your family.

There are many online resources for maps. You can find historical maps, county maps, forestry maps, and more. The Bureau of Land Management www.glorecords.blm.gov has the Official Federal Land patent Records. www.google.maps.com is another great interactive site. You can zoom in or out, change from map to satellite version and more.

Names of places, rivers and even towns have changed over the years. Keep that in mind when looking at new or current maps and at the online maps like 'Google'.

History books

There are thousands of published family and local histories full of information for the genealogist. I was lucky enough to visit a small town in Missouri and at a very small Historical Society they had a county history book. There were several pages full of information about my family from the time the town was founded.

Many libraries have collections of family history books. Large libraries like the Daughters of the American Revolution Library in Washington DC has shelves full of family history books open to the public for research. The number of family histories there is amazing.

Look in books other than just the surname you are researching. You might find your family mentioned in the maiden name of his spouse or in the maiden name of his brother's spouse.

If you find a citation naming a book or publication that is in public domain, meaning the copyright is pre-1923 and has not been renewed, you might be able to find the entire book online. One source is www.google.books.com. Depending on the book you might be able to download the entire thing for free.

www.abebooks.com has many out of print books for sale. You can search by family name, location, historic topic and more. I myself have purchased many books through them of old family histories.

Using Ancestry's card catalog you might find books available for review on line. www.familysearch.org also has many books available for download in PDF format. Any of course there are many other sites.

Military

Military in general

Did your ancestor serve in the military? Do you have a Revolutionary Soldier in the mix? There are several resources to help you.

First, ask your family. Are there any family history stories that tell of great- grandpa being in WWI? Are there any old photos of someone in uniform? What did the obituary say about them? Did it mention military service? Is there a special grave marker? Is there a symbol of some kind on the gravestone indicating military service?

Most records are available through the National Archives and the National Personnel Records Center. However, in 1973 fire destroyed about 80% of the records of veterans discharged from the Army between 1912 and 1960 and a large portion of the Air Force records between 1947 and 1964. One military site to try

Military

is http://www.archives.gov/veterans/military-service-records/. The site has instructions and forms for you to fill out to send for your ancestor's records.

Most of the records of the American Army and Navy were destroyed by fire in 1800 and again in 1814. Efforts have been made to recreate these records from muster rolls, hospital records, prison records, enlistment and discharge papers and pay records. These records are available for the Revolutionary War, the War of 1812 and the Civil War.

Fold3 and Ancestry have many of the military records in their databases. www.fold3.com and www.ancestry.com.

Pensions

The National Archives has the records of pension requests and payments for veterans, their widows or their heirs. Sometimes these records contain a treasure of genealogical information.

Millions of men born between 1873 and 1900 registered for draft for WWI. These are housed at the National Archives. More recent records are still protected by privacy laws.

The National Archives has many branch offices.

Washington, DC Headquarters

800 & Pennsylvania Ave., NW

Washington, DC 20408

202-357-5400 or 1-866-325-7208

Jump Start Your Genealogy Research

www.archives.gov E-mail: inquire@nara.gov

Reference Branch

202-357-5400

Customer Services Center

800-234-8861

Fax: 301-837-0483

NARA—College Park, MD8601 Adelphi Rd.College Park,

MD 20740301-837-2000 or 1-866-272-6272

www.archives.gov

E-mail: inquire@nara.gov

Regional Archives

NARA—Pacific Alaska Region (Anchorage)

654 West Third Ave.

Anchorage, AK 99501-2145

907-261-7800www.archives.gov/pacific-alaska/anchorage/

E-mail: alaska.archives@nara.gov

Serves Alaska

Military

NARA—Pacific Region (Laguna Niguel)

24000 Avila Rd.

Laguna Niguel, CA 92677-3497

949-360-2641

www.archives.gov/pacific/laguna

E-mail: laguna.archives@nara.gov

Serves AZ, Southern CA, and Clark County, NV

NARA—Pacific Region (San Francisco)

1000 Commodore Dr.

San Bruno, CA 94066-2350

650-238-3501www.archives.gov/pacific/san-fransisco

E-mail: sanbruno.archives@nara.govServes northern and central CA, NV (except Clark County), HI, American Samoa, and the Trust Territory of the Pacific Islands.

NARA—Rocky Mountain Region

Denver Federal Center, Building 48

West 6th Ave. and Kipling St.P.O. Box 25307

Denver, CO 80225-0307

303-407-5740

www.archives.gov/rocky-mountain

E-mail: denver.archives@nara.gov

Serves CO, MT, NM, ND, SD, UT, WY

NARA—Southeast Region

5780 Jonesboro Rd.

Morrow, GA 30260-3806

770-968-2100

www.archives.gov/southeast/E-mail: atlanta.archives@nara.gov

Serves AL, FL, GA, KY, MS, NC, SC, TN

NARA—Central Plains Region (Kansas City)

2312 East Bannister Rd.

Kansas City, MO 64131-3011

816-268-8012

www.archives.gov/central plains/kansas cityE-mail: kansascity.archives@nara.gov

Serves AL, FL, GA, KY, MS, NC, SC, TN

NARA—Great Lakes Region

7358 South Pulaski Rd.

Military

Chicago, IL 60629-5898

773-948-9001

www.archives.gov/great-lakes/chicago

E-mail: chicago.archives@nara.gov

Serves IL, IN, MI, MN, OH, WI

NARA—Northeast Region (Boston)

380 Trapelo Rd.

Waltham, MA 02452-6399

866-406-2379

www.archives.gov/northeast/waltham/E-mail: waltham.archives@nara.gov

Serves CT, ME, MA, NH, RI, VT

NARA—Northeast Region (Pittsfield)

10 Conte Dr.

Pittsfield, MA 01201-8230

413-236-3600www.archives.gov/northeast/pittsfield/

E-mail: pittsfield.archives@nara.gov

(Microfilm only)

NARA—Northeast Region (New York City)

201 Varick St., 12th Floor

New York, NY 10014-4811

866-840-1752www.archives.gov/northeast/nyc

E-mail: newyork.archives@nara.gov

Serves NJ, NY, Puerto Rico, and the U.S. Virgin Islands

NARA—Mid Atlantic Region

(Center City Philadelphia)

900 Market St.

Philadelphia, PA 19107-4292

215-606-0100

www.archives.gov/midatlantic/

E-mail: philadelphia.archives@nara.gov

Serves DE, MD, PA, VA, WV

NARA—Southwest Region

501 West Felix St.P.O. Box 6216Ft. Worth, TX 76115-0212

817-831-5620

www.archives.gov/southwest/E-mail: ftworth.archives@nara.gov

Serves AR, LA, OK, TX

NARA—Pacific Alaska Region (Seattle)

Military

6125 Sand Point Way, NE

Seattle, WA 98115-7999

206-336-5115www.archives.gov/pacific-alaska/seattle

E-mail: seattle.archives@nara.govServes ID, OR, WA

Land and Bounty Claims

Land was granted by the government to citizens for their service to their country. These bounty land claims are for service between 1775 and 1855. So, if your ancestor served in the early wars of this country such as the Indian Wars, the Revolutionary War, the War of 1812 or the Mexican War you might find them by searching the bounty land warrant application files. These can also be found at the National Archives.

Organizations

There are several organizations that base their membership on whether or not you can prove your lineage to an ancestor that served in that war. These include organizations like the Daughters of the American Revolution, the Sons of the American Revolution, Daughter or Sons of the Union (Civil War), Ancestors of the Mayflower, Descendants and Founders of New Jersey, the Jamestown Society, the First Georgia Company, just to name a few.

The organizations will assist you in proving your lineage. The Daughters of the American Revolutions Library in Washington, DC has extensive research material to aid you in your search. A local chapter near you will be happy to assist since you will most likely become a member of their chapter.

When looking for a Revolutionary ancestor, remember to look at the big picture. Often relatives joined together. Men could choose which unit they wanted to join and under which officer. They most likely would join under someone they knew or at least heard about from friends or relatives. After the war many of them received their land grants and lived together in the same area. Some of the land grants were in Canada so don't forget to search there. If you don't find much information about your ancestor, study the officer. You may find clues or answers to your questions there.

When you discover the name of the Battalion or Company he served in turn your attention to the history books. Volumes of information have been compiled pertaining to particular battles and the men that fought in them. You will realize what your ancestor went through during that time.

There are also many magazine publications that concentrate on a particular subject such as the Civil War Times, WWII History Magazine, or Military History Magazine. Some are specific to the branch like Air Force Magazine, Army Times, Marine Times or USNI Naval Magazine.

Gravesites

Gravesites may give you a clue that your ancestor served in the military. If there are symbols on the headstone such as a flag, or eagle this could be an indication. Other

Military

symbols might be single or crossed swords, a horse for cavalry, a rifle or cannon might mean artillery.

Look for letters which might show membership in an organization. These may also appear in the obituary. These might include VFW (Veterans of Foreign Wars), USMC (United States Marine Corps) or something similar. A marker placed there by the DAR (Daughters of the American Revolution) or other organization definitely shows military service has been proved.

There are several websites where you can look up what the symbols on the headstone mean. Type 'headstone symbols' in the search engine browser. Here are a few symbols you might see:

1. Anchor: Early Christians used the anchor as a disguised cross, and as a marker to guide the way to secret meeting places.
2. Book: A scholar or book of faith such as the Bible.
3. Butterfly: The soul or resurrection of Christ.
4. Corn: Rebirth or fertility
5. Crossed Swords: Military officer
6. Horseshoe: Protection against evil.
7. Lion: The power of God and protection for the tomb.
8. Rifle: Usually military or hunter
9. Ship: Might mean the person was a sailor.
10. Sunrise: Renewed life

Medical Records

I was not only able to get my father's military service record but his medical records as well. There were pages of information. It is quite a treasure.

You usually need to be a direct relation to obtain the medical records. If you are trying to obtain your uncle's records you may need to get the assistance of your cousin to request them.

Unfortunately almost all of us have been touched by war in some way. Do some research and I think you will most likely find that someone in your tree has served in the military.

You can request military records at http://www.archives.gov/veterans/military-service-records/#evetrecs

Be sure to read the instructions before you begin, in particular the section on who is allowed to request the records and which records may be obtained, and when.

Court Houses

Vital Statistics

Most beginning genealogists already know that the court house is where you go for birth, death and marriage records. However, the Court Houses in the USA hold much more. In other countries these might be referred to as Parish records. In some states it is a separate office of Vital Statistics.

Let's start with the basics of birth, death and marriage records. Start with yourself. Get your documents and they will have the information you need, your mother's maiden name, or maybe your father's occupation.

Vital records are usually the most accurate records you will find. Because it is information gathered by the government, they try to ensure accuracy. The papers are usually filed within days of the event and the people supplying the information are the people involved. They usually know the right answers.

Court Houses

Years ago whether or not you had to register births was left up to the state. Some places required them as early as 1790 and other states like South Carolina didn't require it until 1915. Many of our early settlers lived far from any city and they weren't about to make the long journey just to register a birth. Most births at that time were at home and that was good enough for them. The government didn't need to know. It was none of their business.

If you are going to visit the court house, make a plan and set goals. Prepare your research log and bring your charts. Calls ahead, write or go online and just type in your state and 'vital statistics' and you will probably be supplied with the link to that site. Read it. They might tell you something like the following from the Kentucky Office of Vital Statistics web site.

Office of Vital Statistics

275 East Main Street 1E-A

Frankfort, KY 40621

(502) 564-4212

Kentucky's Vital Statistics Law, enacted by the General Assembly in 1910, provides for and legalizes the registration of births and deaths.

The Office of Vital Statistics does not have records of births or deaths prior to 1911, except delayed records of births for those born before 1911 which have been established by affidavits and documentary evidence.

Central registration of marriages and divorces began in Kentucky in June 1958. The Office of Vital Statistics does not have records of marriages or divorces prior to 1958. To inquire about marriage certificates prior to June 1958, please call the **county clerk** in the county where the marriage license was issued. To inquire about divorce certificates prior to June 1958, please call the **circuit county clerk** that granted the divorce decree.

The Kentucky Department for Libraries and Archives, P.O. Box 537, 300 Coffee Tree Road, Frankfort, KY 40602, (502) 564-8300, has birth and death records for the cities of Louisville, Lexington, Covington and Newport, which enacted records collection ordinances before 1911. KDLA also has birth and death records (statewide coverage) prior to 1911 and 1911-1957 death records (statewide coverage).

This information has told you right off the bat that if you are looking for information prior to 1911 you should not be looking at the Office of Vital Statistics but to look at the Kentucky Department for Libraries and Archives.

The site also gives contact information and directions. All of this may have saved you time or a trip to the wrong office.

Adoption Records

Other types of records that might be available at a court house are adoption records. However, these records are difficult to obtain. There are organizations that assist you. The Adoptee's Liberty Movement Association is one of them.

Rootsweb has a great resource for adoptees. http://www.rootsweb.ancestry.com/~rwguide/lesson31.htm?cj=1&netid=cj&o_xid=0001029688&o_lid=0001029688&o_sch=Affiliate+External

Another site is www.adoption.com. This site helps to reunite biological families.

Genealogy Today provides many articles and resources. http://www.genealogytoday.com/adoption/puzzle//?

Death Records

Death records are completed almost immediately after the death by someone who was there. However, the information is usually provided by a relative or friend so it may not be accurate. You will find the person's name, date and place of death, age, cause of death, date and perhaps place of birth, current residence, occupation, parent names and maybe even their birth places, the spouses name and the maiden name for the wife, burial place, funeral home, the doctor, and even some witnesses.

You can also learn more about a person's death from the Social Security Death Index. This is a database of names, birth and death dates for millions of Americans. It is available online.

The data include:

- Given name and surname; and since the 1990s, middle initial
- Date of birth
- Month and year of death; or full date of death for accounts active in 2000 or later
- Social Security number
- State or territory where the Social Security number was issued
- Last place of residence while the person was alive (ZIP code)
- Once a deceased person is found in the database, the person's application for Social Security card (Form SS-5) can be ordered from the Social Security Administration. The SS-5 may contain additional genealogical data, such as birthplace, father's name, and mother's full maiden name or in some cases that information may be unavailable.

You can search the SSDI online at several websites including Ancestry.com.

Marriage Records

Marriage records of course give you information about the bride and groom. Years ago exact legal names were not required. They may have used a nickname or if they were known by their middle name they might have used it. The document will also list the parents.

Besides the marriage licenses, ask if they have the marriage 'application' on file. Often the application has more details. Some states will let you view these and some will not.

Divorce Records

Divorce records are found at the court house too. These records will list both of the individual's names, including the maiden name of the woman. You will most likely find information about the marriage (when and where), birth dates and places, names of children along with birth information and of course the information pertaining to the divorce itself.

There might be property settlements. You might find they owned land in another state. Then comes the question, why? This leads to further research. Is that where one of them lived prior to the marriage? Are there relatives still living there? Did they purchase this land after marriage? Did they inherit it?

Immigration or Emigration

What's the difference?

Emigrant and Immigrant are often incorrectly used. An emigrant leaves their land to live in another country. An Immigrant is a person who once resided somewhere else and now lives in your country. I try to remember it as Emigrant starts with 'E' and that person is 'E' ending their relationship with their country. Immigrant, starting with 'I' represents 'IN', they are now 'IN' this country.

New Immigrants in this country might have filed a Declaration of Intention to become a citizen. In the 19th century they could file as soon as they came to this country. But often they filed and then picked up roots and moved again. These papers may not be filed in the area they ultimately settled in. They had to wait at least 2 years after filing the Declaration of Intent before filing papers for citizenship or be a resident for 5 years. Usually only men applied for citizenship.

Depending upon the location and time period of the naturalization, records may be located at the local or county court, in a state or regional archives facility, at the National Archives, or through U.S. Citizenship and Immigration Services. Some naturalization indexes and digitized copies of original naturalization records are also starting to become available online.

Many immigrants filed the first papers and never followed through with becoming citizens. Depending on the year or where they lived they may have realized that they could live here, work their farms, and run their businesses without having to become a citizen. It may have been a long hard trip to the proper court and they couldn't afford it or couldn't afford to take the time away from their farms and businesses.

The Federal Census of 1900 was the first to indicate a person's status with 'P' for 1st papers filed, "Na" for naturalized citizen and "Al" for alien (who filed no papers).

Until 1922 a woman automatically became a citizen when her husband did. Any children under 21 also became citizens. However, none of this was cast in stone and there were always exceptions or loose interpretations of the law. Before 1906 naturalization papers could have been filed at any court such as municipal, county, state or federal court. Therefore, you might have to check all of these locations.

Court Houses

Naturalization papers might include name, nationality, age, birth date, port of departure, arrival date, port of entry, physical description or in later years even a photo. Some may include the town they originated from in their country. Standard forms were introduced in 1906. Sometimes all that was used prior to 1906 was a large log book. There was no literacy requirement. You ancestor might have signed with an 'X'.

The U.S. Citizenship and Immigration Service – USCIS (formerly known as the INS) is where to look for files after September 1906 at http://www.uscis.gov/ . They are headquartered in Washington, DC. Requests can take several months to process so you might find it quicker to look at online digitized sources.

 In many states you might not have been able to own land unless you had filed a declaration of intent. In 1862 the Homestead Act allowed only citizens to own land. If your ancestor obtained land through the Homestead Act then you have a clue to search further. They had to be a citizen. Look for their citizenship papers.

Going back further to the colonial time period you have to understand that this was NOT the United States. England owned the land. English born citizens did not need to take Oaths of Allegiance; they were already citizens of England. Acts of naturalization had to come from Parliament and the Crown.

In 1657/58 the Virginia General Assembly passed an act letting foreigners become 'denizens', (or subjects) of the colony of Virginia. These individuals must have lived in the colony for four years and were required to take an Oath of Fidelity.

Therefore, if you find a record of your ancestor taking the Oath of Fidelity or Allegiance after 1657/58 you could look for records of their arrival four years (or more) prior to that time.

In 1709 Parliament passed an act for the naturalization of foreign-born Protestants. Three years later there was a flood of Germans emigrating from the Palatine area of Germany. It was later repealed.

In 1740, Parliament passed another act. This one was not exclusive to Virginia. This act required that the applicant had to have resided a minimum of seven years in the colonies. Applicants were required to take an Oath of Allegiance and a promise to follow the Christian faith.

Oaths often required the signatures of witnesses which may lead to additional clues about your ancestor.

Ship Records

Although ship records are NOT held at the courthouse they bear mentioning in this section about Immigration Records.

Many people only think of Ellis Island in New York, when they think of ancestors immigrating to America. There were many more ports of entry such as Baltimore, Philadelphia or Boston. Or perhaps they didn't enter at an eastern port at all. Maybe they landed in New Orleans, Seattle or in Alaska. They might have landed in Canada first, and later came across the border. Check their records. After immigrating to Canada they may have entered the USA through one of our northern cities such as Detroit.

Court Houses

From 1855 – 1890 they came through Castle Garden in New York, known then as Castle Clinton. At that time it was up to the states to handle immigration and immigration records. It wasn't until the Immigration Act of 1882 that the federal government voted to be the controlling body over this process. Ellis Island opened in 1892.

The Ellis Island web site has a large database of the immigrants that landed and were processed through their facility. 1/3 of all Americans most likely have an ancestor that was processed through Ellis Island. www.ellisisland..org

Castle Garden has information on over 10 million immigrants from 1830 – 1892. www.castlegarden.org

Many passengers did not survive the passage. These individuals were buried upon arrival. For example, if your relative died and passed through immigration at Castle Island they might be buried at Hart's Island.

There are many web sites to research and find ships records. http://www.archives.gov/research/immigration/ is a good place to start.

Ship records may indicate where the person sailed from, who he sailed with, and his final destination. Many of the larger libraries also have volumes of books that list passenger arrivals. Passenger lists provide that personal link to the old country.

Court

Your ancestor might have been involved in a court case. They may have given testimony or been a witness. You will most likely have to look at an index and find the case number and then you find the copy of the case documentation. You might find these in local courts but don't forget the state and federal court system too.

Or was your ancestor the one on trial? You might find out that you had a jailbird in the family. You need to know something about the crime, such as the location and about the time it occurred. This will give you the information about the jurisdiction and the type of court records you need to search. Court records of criminal cases are public records and anyone may look at them unless the person was underage or the records were sealed for some other reason.

Often families, especially the older generation, don't want to talk about someone's incarceration. It is an embarrassment to the family. Find out as much as you can.

I found that one of my uncles happened to be the only young man of legal age when the group decided to steal a tire from a mining company. He was the only one that served time for the crime. I found the records at the state historical society. The courts no longer had room to store such old documents. There was an index, I found his name and the rest was easy.

The papers may help you find out where they went to prison. Prison records might give you a record of visitors, or tell you about their behavior.

I had another ancestor from the colonial time period that paid his court fine in bushels of tobacco.

Be sensitive with this information. The rest of your family might not think it's as 'cool' as you do. They may be embarrassed and may not be too pleased with you if you share this information with the world. If the person is still living you most certainly should discuss it with them.

If there is a criminal record remember to check the newspapers during that time. You might find them in the headlines. Check with local law libraries, they may have more recent cases in their data base.

Land / Deed Records

Land Deed Records are another court house gem. There are many online sources but nothing beats going to the local court house. I can tell you most of your ancestors at some point owned land. They bought, sold, or left it in Wills.

Deed books are kept at courthouses usually with the Registrar of Deeds. A land grant is when the government transferred the land to the first person to own the land. Deeds transfer property from one person to another. Wills will transfer land to the heirs and this is written on the deed. Some people may have kept copies of their deed or 'abstract' in their possession.

When you go to the courthouse to search deeds you will start with the index. The staff will most likely help you. There are different indexes. There is the index of the person selling the land or the 'grantor' and then there is the index of the buyer or the 'grantee'. Courthouses are different so don't be afraid to ask how their deeds are indexed.

The indexes will give you more information as to what book and page number you will find the deed in, or the specific Deed Book. Sometimes you can look at the actual deed and other times it might be on microfilm. Local historical societies or libraries might already have copies on microfilm.

The language on the deeds might scare you off but slow down and read it and it isn't so bad. It just looks daunting. It will name the dates, the people involved. It might mention that this is a son or a wife. You'll find out how much they paid for the land or if it was transferred as a gift to a family member or willed to the widow. You might even see their signatures at the end.

As stated earlier, there is going to be a legal description of the land. This is where those plat maps come in handy. You know what I mean - the NW ¼ of the NE ¼ of Section 12, T10N, R8W, 160 acres. The easiest thing to do is start from the end and word backwards. The description is 160 acres that are in Range 8 West, which is in Township 10 North, which is in Section 12. Section 12 is divided into fourths. Locate the NE quarter and from that quarter find the NW quarter. There is your land. It is much easier to see on a land map and the staff will assist you. Once you see it in picture or map form it makes much more sense.

In some of old records I found for my family the government hadn't divided the land up in such a precise manor. It might say: A line from Elmer Johnson's mill, following Skunk Creek to the Pine Ridge, or something similar. This can be a bit more difficult to determine the exact location but it can be done. This type of land description is called 'Metes and Bounds'.

Metes and bounds is a way of describing the land by using physical land marks and descriptions as well as directions and distances. This system has been used in England for centuries and therefore was used in the original Thirteen Colonies that went on to become the United States.

Land records within a city will probably list things by lot and block number.

Taxes

Your ancestor might have been missed in all of the other documents you look at but you can be sure that the tax collector didn't miss them. Whether it was land tax or personal property tax the government wanted their money. If they registered to vote they are listed on tax records.

You might find your ancestors full name, residence, how many males lived in the house, how much livestock they owned or farmland, if they owned slaves, and amount of acreage they owned.

I could not find any records of property that one of my relatives owned. However, tax records indicated that he was a tenant farmer and he did owe tax on personal property. He had been a tenant farmer all of his life.

There were taxes paid called tithables to the church. There were Poll taxes to be paid for every man and a tax for every slave or servant that was paid by the parent or owner.

Delinquent taxes might have been printed in the local newspapers so check that section of the paper.

Around Town

Employment Records

Employment records are often an overlooked source of information. Many large companies keep these records for years. Others donate them to the local historical societies.

While visiting Anaconda, Montana one year I discovered that the historical society had many of the old employment records from the mining companies during the early 1900's. I was able to find a relative's employment history and a company photograph! I also learned a great deal about his occupation and how mining was done back in those early years.

Some companies also print a collection of their company history on an anniversary. Say, 50 years in business or something like that.

Clubs, Societies, and Organizations are another place in town to look. There aren't as many ethnic clubs as there used to be but some areas still have the Old Italian Hall or other ethnic hall. If they don't the records might be at the local library or historical society. I found information on my family in such records.

Churches

Church records are kept for years. They may be old books with birth, baptisms, confirmations, marriages, deaths and more. They often produce a history book to celebrate an anniversary and your relative may have posed for a picture. Many churches also create a photographic directory of its members every so many years.

Older church records may indicate whether or not they paid their tithe or in some cases whether or not they were punished or banished for a period of time.

Many of these church records have been transcribed and are in print (books), genealogical magazines (i.e. Western Maryland Genealogy) and available online.

Cemeteries

Where there is a church there is usually a cemetery. However, some cemeteries are government run, by the city or county.

There is usually a caretaker of the cemetery. Find out who this person is ahead of time if possible and let them know what gravesites you are looking for. Hopefully they will have detailed maps of the burial plots and who is buried where. This is a big help. You don't want to spend all day trudging around a huge cemetery looking for your ancestor's headstone.

Things to bring with you: paper, pencil, soft brush, stiff brush, rag, spray bottle of water, a small shovel or garden shovel and grass clippers. It's best to visit cemeteries in the spring and fall if it is a small neglected sight. Branches and low growing plants or brush won't be as overwhelming as in the summer. If it is well maintained then spring, summer or fall are great. Wear long pants to protect against ticks and scratches. You may be on your knees cleaning a headstone. Wear sturdy shoes and bring a pair of gloves. Long sleeves if it is very rural as you might encounter a swarm of mosquitoes. Bring a hat to keep out the sun.

Ask for a map of the plots if possible. You might see names of relatives or family friends buried nearby. If a map isn't available create your own while you are still there making sure to indicate landmarks and roads.

Write down the names, dates and inscriptions exactly as you see them. Use the brush and rag to clean off the stone. Use the garden shovel and clippers to remove any overgrowth. Do this carefully so as not to damage the stone. If you are having difficulty reading the stone use the spray bottle of water and wet the headstone. The letters seem to pop out and are much easier to read.

Take a photograph. Take several. Take one far away to show landmarks. Take several more getting closer with each shot. Take close up shots of just sections of the headstone. Don't forget the back of the stone. Often there is more information written there. You might also want a photo of the front gates.

Around Town

This is where digital cameras come in handy. You can see immediately if the photos turned out. Be aware of where the sun is and any shadows being cast.

Look around. Sometimes there are family member close by. One section of a cemetery I visited had 5 children from the same family buried in a row. When I got back to the library I looked up records and found out that an influenza epidemic had spread through the area that year.

Once in awhile you may find out that the cemetery your ancestor is buried in is on private property. Please make sure you ask permission before entering. Ask at the local historical society or library and they will often know of small private cemeteries.

Sadly most of the really old cemeteries have been neglected or abandoned. They may be overgrown with weeds and trees and difficult to find. If you suspect from your research that there might be a family burial plot at a certain location and you can't find it try these tips.

- Look for higher ground. They avoided low lying areas that might be prone to flooding.
- Look for a large old tree or the remains of one.
- Look for 'raised' or 'sunken' areas in the earth. The gravesites often left small mounds or indentations. If you see several small mounds in a row this may indicate the gravesites of several family members.
- Consider hiring a professional researcher. Historians and human remain dogs can sometimes find what you can't.

Sometimes the local historical/genealogical societies may have mapped and indexed the site or local libraries might have the information.

For years the location of the burial within the cemetery was of importance and signified the person's status in the community. Your status in life determined many things such as whether or not you were buried within the churchyard's boundaries or outside the boundaries.

Distinction was within the churchyard and generally on the east side to have the best view of the rising sun on Judgment Day. A less desirable location would be on the south side and even further down the ladder of distinction would be the north side or 'Devil's' area.

Military cemeteries are located in almost every State, as well as in foreign countries. There are over 200 cemeteries established by the Federal government for the burial of war casualties and veterans. One of the best known is the Arlington Cemetery in Arlington, VA

Grave deeds are given for ownership of a specific grave plot. Check with the cemetery to see if there are copies of the application forms or deeds.

There are places online to learn about doing gravestone rubbings. Many people enjoy doing this and taking home the artwork. There are even videos on YouTube.

There is a service online www.findagrave.com where you can browse by location, date, or name. You can join the organization and volunteer to photograph graves for someone that doesn't live in your area. It's easy.

Around Town

They send in a request and if the cemetery is in your area you take the photos and post them for the requestor. You can request the assistance of someone to photograph a grave site if you are unable to travel to the location. Everybody helps everybody. Nice.

Along with churches and cemeteries come Funeral homes. Funeral homes and morticians may have on record the burial location. If it is an obscure location they have to know how to get there.

City directories may list the undertaker for the year you are researching and local historical societies or state repositories may have those records.

The International Cemetery Cremation and Funeral Association is a place to look for help. This group formed in 1887. https://www.iccfa.com

There are other associations like the Jewish Cemetery Association of North America, Ohio Cemetery Association (and many other states), or religious groups such as the Catholic Cemetery Association.

Some city directories may be found on a website http://www.uscitydirectories.com .

Schools

Another place to look around town is the at the school and alumni records. School libraries usually have copies of all of the year books. You might find enrollment and transcript records. Some schools or universities have alumni newsletters. You could research old copies, or submit a request for information in their next issue. There might also be fraternity, sorority or reunion records. Some of the old records may have been donated to the local library or historical society.

At a historical society I found records indicating my great aunt taught at a small rural country school in South Dakota and 4 of her 11 students were related to her. You may also find them listed as a 'boarder' on a census record for that time period. Teachers often boarded with one of the local families.

If your ancestor went to a college or university check their websites. They may have a section for genealogical researchers or at the least an address where you can write to and see if they have such records. They might also have history books written about the school. Your ancestor might have been captain of the debate team or homecoming queen!

City Directories

Even before telephones and telephone books there were City Directories. The directories listed people and businesses in the town and surrounding area.

Directories list the address and often the occupation of the primary resident. I have found many of my relatives in these directories and then drove by the old addresses. Some homes are still standing and some were long ago torn down. However, check with the historical societies again. Many of them have photographs and your ancestor's house just might be one of them.

Prisons/ Hospitals / Institutions

Was your ancestor ever in trouble with the law? You might find out that you had a criminal in the family. The nearest prison to where they lived might be a source of information. Depending on the crime it could be a local prison, state or federal prison.

You need to know something about the crime, such as the location and about the time it occurred. This will give you the information about the jurisdiction and the type of court records you need to search. Court records of criminal cases are public records and anyone may look at them unless the person was underage or the records were sealed for some other reason.

Perhaps your ancestor was tried, convicted and sent to jail in the late 1700's for stealing a loaf of bread. Maybe he inadvertently let his mare breed with the neighbor's stallion without paying a fee. Maybe he was in a brawl at a local pub or struck his wife.

Institutions are often listed at the end of a census record. Prisons, Orphanages, Almshouse, Poorhouse, Work Houses, Mental Hospitals and Insane Asylums may be where your ancestor resided. Included in this list might be Old Homes for the elderly or military unable to take care of themselves. There were also religious 'institutions' run by the churches.

Search the files of the local probate court, which normally handles guardianships and legal papers to have someone 'committed'.

Museums

Local museums are such fun. I love spending time in museums. I'm a museum junky! Not only do I like the normal Historical Museums but there may be a

Newspaper Museum, or the Great Lakes Museum or just about any topic.

They all have information and archives that might help you. In Michigan I visited a small Finnish museum and found out that they were the ones that had all of the employment records for the mining companies located there. Most of the population at the time was of Finnish descent.

If you are visiting an area try going to www.maps.google.com and enter the city and state. Then click on 'search nearby' and type in museum. You can easily find any museums in the area.

Reenactments

Attend Reenactments in the area. You know the ones like the 'Shoot out at the OK Corral' in Tombstone or the Civil War reenactments in Virginia or tour old forts and homesteads.

You will see period clothing, weapons, tools, living conditions and so much more. You can put yourself in your ancestor's shoes and almost smell the gun smoke.

Some locations have complete working settlements built to show us what life was like during that time period. You can stop in an see a woman baking, a man with a foot powered lathe making a table or a tailor's shop.

Take notes and you can add this information to your family's story. These places usually have books that also help you discover what life was like during that time period.

Culture

Which brings to mind, what was the culture like at the time? What type of tools did they use? What kinds of jobs did they hold? For example my ancestor was a cooper by trade. A cooper was someone that made wooden barrels and tubs.

Did your ancestor live on a farm? What kinds of crops did they farm? In early Virginia tobacco was the main crop. Tobacco was like money. There was not a lot of printed money or coins to be had. You could use tobacco to purchase things from merchants. Taxes were even paid in tobacco. Court fines were paid in tobacco.

English merchants supplied colonists with manufactured goods and took their profits primarily from the return cargoes of tobacco.

From the first, Virginia resembled England in the development of a feudal system. Men of no special status held estates of ten, twenty, or thirty thousand acres. This was the result of the rapid increase in the cultivation of tobacco.

For a great many years the white servants were much more numerous than the blacks. Many were indentured servitude, meaning someone paid their passage or provided room and board for them in exchange for servitude for a determined number of years, 7, 14 20, it varied. This was equal to slavery in all points except the blacks were slaves for eternity.

This created great differences in the classes of citizens unknown in the New England colonies, all because of tobacco. So, tobacco was responsible for Virginia's social and political conditions.

Early homes had fireplaces but no chimney only a hole in the roof to let the smoke out. How did they preserve their food at the time? Did they salt it, dry it or did they have ice boxes? Could they purchase manufactured goods? Were the goods made in this country or were they imported like the molasses imports from the Dutch colonies in the West Indies during the early colonial days.

Who was in power? Was it King George of England? Who was president? What was the political atmosphere like? Were they at war? Was there rationing like in the 1940's?

Did they have radio or television yet or did they rely on town meetings and town criers for their news?

What had or hadn't been invented yet? Did they have electricity yet? Did they even have toothbrushes?

How did they travel; by foot along animal trails or by covered wagon? Did they make long journeys by train?

What was the life expectancy at that time? Did people normally live to be 45 or 50 and if you ancestor lived to be 65 was he considered unusual?

There are so many, many questions you can ask and find the answers to that will give life to the story of your ancestors. Take the time to research these types of questions and turn your facts into story.

Technology

Where to begin?

Technology as exploded in recent years and it has made the genealogist's research hours much more productive. There are hundreds; I should say thousands, of web sites dedicated to genealogy research of some type.

Let's start with what you have at home. Most of you probably have a computer. If you have a laptop that's great! Although there is an occasional library that won't let you use your laptop on their premises most places do allow it. Instead of lugging armloads of files and charts you can have it all at your fingertips with your laptop.

Printers are a must of course if you have a computer. You will be printing out forms, completed group sheets, research logs, and so on.

I remember years ago when I started my research there were no computers and home scanners. Many people are reluctant to let you take their photos out of their

Technology

possession. I had to beg and promise that I would return them as soon as possible and that I would guard them with my life.

So, try to get a scanner. If you are lucky enough to obtain or borrow family documents or photos you can scan them right to your hard drive and return them unblemished.

This should be a flatbed scanner. You can't feed photos or precious documents through a feed type scanner. My kids bought me a flatbed scanner for about $75 for my birthday a few years ago. It's great!

Mine is a Visioneer flatbed scanner that will accommodate legal size documents. It's as about the depth of a laptop but longer of course to handle legal size. However, it has fit nicely in my backpack right next to the laptop.

I also have a Flip Pal. I like this for smaller photos and documents. It does have the capability to 'stitch' the document together after you have taken the scan but to me that adds another step to the process that I don't have to do with my Visioneer.

I often take my scanner with me when I visit relatives and as we are going through photos and old papers I am scanning as we go. It also helps me with my accuracy. The people I am interviewing are right there to assist me in labeling and recording the story behind the photograph and they don't have to let go of their cherished photos.

You can enter the information they are giving you directly into your software. There are many, many choices for genealogy software. Legacy, Family Tree Maker, Roots Magic, and Ancestral Quest are just a few and sell for around $30.00.

These programs allow you to export your data to a GEDCOM file. GEDCOM is more or less a generic database file. GEDCOM files allow you to share your database with others or use it in a different program.

Software makes record keeping so much easier. After you enter your ancestor you can add all of their details such as spouse, children, marriage, death, and so on. You can view individuals or family groups, add a source citation, photos and scanned documents.

Some have map features so you can track you ancestor's movements or see how many lived near each other. You can do searches by name, place, and so on. You can print pedigree charts, descendent charts, family group sheets, and various other reports, in just seconds. Some have the function to create a book or other ways to share your family's history.

Digital cameras are the way to go. You have instant results letting you know if your photograph turned out or not. How devastated would you be to travel 600 miles, take photos of gravestones, historic homes, or family members only to find out later that some of them didn't turn out. Digital cameras have come way down in price and you can get a small, 'stick in your purse or pocket' kind for around $75-$100.

I always have my camera set to the highest resolution possible. This helps assure that my pictures are crisp and clear. It does make for larger files but you can

Technology

always reduce a file for e-mailing. A poor quality photo can't be improved no matter how hard you try.

Some Smart Phones now take excellent pictures as well. However, the storage is usually limited and often the resolution is not a crisp and clear as the camera would take.

This is not going to be a lesson on taking digital photographs. I do have a few suggestions though. Check your lighting. You don't want people squinting into the sun or in dark shadows. Get up close. You want to see what the person looks like. You don't really need the trees in the background or the person's feet in the picture.

Straight on shots are not flattering. Have the subject turn slightly sideways, turn their head toward you, lift their chin a bit and drop their shoulders. I don't know what it is about getting your picture taken that makes people stiffen up like a board, puff out their chest and create a double chin for themselves.

As I stated earlier, if at a cemetery and taking photographs of headstones, take several. Take one far away to show landmarks. Take several more getting closer with each shot. Take close up shots of just sections of the headstone. Don't forget the back of the stone. Often there is more written there. You might also want a photo of the front gates.

This goes for any houses, churches, neighborhoods, country sides, monuments and more. Take the best quality and make the quantity enough that you have several representations of the subject to choose from.

Have a notebook and take notes of what you are photographing. Write down full names, birth dates, who's related to whom. Write down everything that is on the gravestone. Even with all of your care in taking the photograph you still might have trouble reading a faded stone.

Videos are a good idea. Video record interviews, they will be treasures to keep. It helps you get the facts straight when you get home and try to transcribe your notes.

If you don't have a video camera most of the digital cameras have a short video function. You can video tape 30 second bits of family members and add them to your genealogy records. This does eat up a lot of memory in the camera though.

Some video cameras now have the capability to extract still photos from the video. What a wonderful concept.

If you don't have video capabilities when interviewing use a voice recorder. There are many inexpensive digital recorders on the market. After you are done recording you can easily load the entire recording onto your computer and use them to make CD/DVD family histories by adding the voice to a photo slide show.

Resources Online

Volumes could be written for all of the online genealogical sites. Some are searchable databases, some are 'how to', some are craft ideas. You can type just about anything into the search engine with the word 'genealogy' and you will find sites for you to start researching. For example, I typed in 'Norwegian genealogy records' in Google and got over 1500 sites.

Do plenty of internet searches with key words for your family, area, county, state, country, ethnicity, and so on. There are history centers, societies, preservation projects and many people that are continuously posting new information online. You might want to try message boards. These are sites where you can query surnames or post them asking if anyone has any information to share.

Online resources are plentiful. I will just highlight a few. This is by no means even a small fraction of the sites available. I've already given you many throughout this book. However, I'll give you some more examples so you know the variety available.

To list all of them would be impossible and like I said, it would fill volumes. I just want to give you a sampling or idea of the variety of websites available. You'll have to take it from there and just do a variety of searches.

NOTE: Some sites require a membership fee, others are free.

Just a few website samples:

About Genealogy: http://genealogy.about.com

A variety of information on various topics

African-American Genealogy Group: www.aagg.org

African-American research

Allen County Public Library: www.acpl.lib.in.us

One of the leading genealogy departments in a public library

Ancestors on Board: www.ancestorsonboard.com

Records on people leaving England

Ancestry: www.ancestry.com

26,000 databases with billions of indexed names and digitized records - DNA center, knowledge library, book creation, photos, and so much more

Angel Island.org: www.angel-island.org

Records on the processing of Asian Immigrants through Angel Island in San Francisco Bay

Bureau of Land Management: www.blm.gov

Database of land records

Canadian Genealogy Centre: www.collectionscanada.gc.ca/genealogy

Technology

Immigration and naturalization databases, vital census, military and land records

Castle Garden: www.castlegarden.org

Immigrant arrival records from ship manifests

Cyndi's List: www.cyndislist.com

Extensive index to genealogical resources on the internet. From A-Z and country to country

East European Family History: http://feefhs.org

The Federation of East European Family History Societies has materials dealing with Eastern Europe.

Ellis Island: www.ellisisland.org

Immigrant arrival records from ship manifests

European Search Engine: NedGen: www.nedgen.com

Search engine for online family trees in Europe

Family History 101: www.familyhistory101.com

Census, military, land, court, vital, probate, church, cemetery, taxes

Family Search: www.familysearch.org

A billion names in searchable database (owned by the Church of Jesus Christ of Latter-day Saints

Fold3: www.fold3.com

Digitized records, name database, documents, Revolutionary War, Civil War, and more

Genealogy Bank: www.genealogybank.com

Newspapers, books, obituaries, historical documents

Genealogy.com: www.genealogy.com

Searchable database, learning center, create your family tree online.

GenLookups: www.genlookups.com

Searchable database and volunteers that will look up information for you at their location

Technology

GenSoftware Review: http://genealogy-software-review.toptenreviews.com

Review of the top 10 genealogy software

Heritage Quest: www.heritagequestonline.com

Digitized books, searchable database by surname

Hispanic Genealogy: www.hispanicgen.org

Links to Hispanic genealogy by the Colorado Society of Hispanic Genealogy

Historical Map Collection: www.davidrumsey.com

David Rumsey Historical Map Collection of over 18,000 maps

Homestead national Monument of America: www.nps.gov

Database of homestead records from Nebraska land office

How to Trace Indian Ancestry: www.doi.gov/ancestry.html

U.S. Department of Interior's website on tracing your Indian ancestry

Jump Start Your Genealogy Research

Library of Congress: www.loc.gov

Largest library in the world. Millions of books, recordings, photographs, maps and more

Live Roots: www.liveroots.com

Database of genealogical resources

Mayflower History: www.mayflowerhistory.com

Deals with the Mayflower, Pilgrims and Plymouth colony

Missouri Digital Heritage: www.sos.mo.gov/mdh

Searchable database of newspapers, soldiers, photos and more

National Archives: www.archives.gov

Databases on a variety of topics - when you find what you are looking for you can order it or do an interlibrary loan

National Genealogical Society: www.ngsgenealogy.org

Society of people interested in genealogy

Technology

Newberry Library: www.newberry.org

Extensive genealogy library in Chicago

Newspaper Archives: www.newspaperarchive.com

Database of historical newspapers

Olive Tree Genealogy: www.olivetreegenealogy.com

Ships Passenger Lists to the USA, Canada and South Africa

Orphan Trains: www.orphantraindepot.com

Information about the Orphan Trains from 1854-1929

Revolutionary War Pension Files: www.heritagequstonline.com

Images pertaining to participation in the Revolutionary War

Roots Web: www.rootsweb.org

Owned by Ancestry.com with a variety of searchable databases

Slave Voyages: www.slavevoyages.org

Database on 35,000 slaving voyages.

Social Security Death Index: www.SSDI.archives.com

Database of Social Security records

Trans Atlantic Slave Trade Database: www.slavevoyages.org

Database of slave voyages between 1544 and 1866

West Virginia Division of Culture and History: www.wvculture.org

Birth, death and marriage records back to 1784

World Vital Records: www.worldvitalrecords.com

Digital books, newspapers, passenger lists, census, gravestone

Citations/Questionnaires/Forms

Citations

Learn to record correct citations right from the start. This will make it much easier in the future to find records you are looking for. It provides consistency and ensures accuracy.

A source citation is recording where you obtained the information such as document, newspaper article, the person themselves, and so on.

There are primary and secondary sources. A primary source is one of good quality such as a birth record if it was recorded at the time of the birth when both parents were present and were giving accurate information about themselves and the newborn. A secondary source is a source that was created well after the fact. My grandfather's birth was not recorded at the time of the

Citations/Questionnaires/Forms

birth but recorded years later by his sister for legal reasons. This is a secondary source.

There are original and derivative source. Original sources are of course just what they say, the original document or photo, or article. A derivative source is a photo copy, or a transcription, a summarization or something similar.

There is no specific right way to make your citations unless you are trying to become a board certified genealogist. In that case they have standards you must follow. However, there are some well accepted ways of recording citations.

Book: title, author, all of the publishing information such as date, name of publisher, location, etc. If there is more than one volume you should include the volume number, and. page number. Where did you find it? (Library name, location, etc.)

A great site to help you create citations is www.easybib.com. You can enter information for websites, books, and more. After you enter the information it will create the citation for you. Then just copy and paste it into your document or database notes.

For example I clicked the tab for books and entered information for the website www.abebooks.com and it created "Search Thousands of Booksellers Selling Millions of New & Used Books." *AbeBooks Official Site.* N.p., n.d. Web. 24 Feb. 2014.

For another I entered under the books tab, 'Elizabeth Shown Mills'. Several of her books were displayed in a list. I chose the one I wanted and it created the citation as follows: Mills, Elizabeth Shown. *Evidence Explained: Citing History Sources from Artifacts to Cyberspace.* Baltimore, MD: Genealogical Pub., 2007. Print. It's GREAT!

When using an online database they most often will provide the citation for you. All you have to do is copy and paste it into your research. If you're using Ancestry's little green leaf it will add it for you.

When I am at a library and photocopy portions of reference books, family histories, and so on I always copy the title page and whatever page the library has put their numbering system on.

At the end of the day I ask if I can borrow any of their stamps and ink pads that have the name of the library and if possible the address. I flip all of my papers over and stamp the back of every single one. It saves me a lot of writing, I know where I got the document and if a page gets misplaced I can easily find where it goes.

Sometimes I print labels up ahead of time and adhere them to the back of the pages. These are just the run of the mill address type labels that you peel and stick. The labels may include:

Location: _____

Address: _____

Phone: _____

Source: _____

Volume: _____

Citations/Questionnaires/Forms

Page: _____

If possible I might put the librarian's name that helped me. If I need additional pages he or she might remember me if I call back and be just as helpful.

Microfilm: series and roll. Again, if you printed anything mark on the back where you got it.

Birth/Death/Marriage Records: Where did you find it? Is it an original from the courthouse or is it a photo copy from an internet database? Give the URL address and any other information about the website so you can find it again if need be.

Newspapers: Name of newspaper, date, page, column and paragraph. Give the library, location or website of the newspaper source. If photocopying newspapers it is easy to get wrapped up in the article and print only that. Try to print enough of the page so it shows the title, date, and page number. Then zoom in and print another copy of just the article.

When entering data into your software program or family group sheets you need to site the sources as you enter it. Don't think, 'I'll go back and do it later'. It never happens. If you don't have room on the front of the family group sheet write it on the back referencing the item you are sourcing.

Cemeteries: Try to site the location as exactly as you can. What road, row and how many headstones over. Of course get the name, address, phone of the cemetery and the name of the caretaker if possible.

Surnames should be all in Upper Case letters, Vickie Lynn CHUPURDIA. It makes it so much easier when reviewing documents to catch the surnames easily. Always list the woman's maiden name, not her married name. If the person was well known by a nickname you can enter that in quotes after the given name. Be sure to record alternate spellings.

Locations should be smallest to largest such as city, county, state, country. For example: Duluth, St. Louis County, Minnesota, USA.

Boundaries change many times. Know the history of the location and write it as it was at the time, such as West Virginia didn't become a state until 20 June 1863. Any records prior to that should say Virginia.

Most genealogy software will let you choose the date format you would like to use but the preferred style is Day/ Month/Year (smallest to largest). 15 Jan 1902, 15 JAN 1902, or 15 January 1902.

If doing research in countries other than the USA you will find that most of them use this format. The USA is one of the few countries that use Month/Day/Year as a normal way of writing the date. This could easily lead to confusion. Is 9/8/1880 September 8th or the 9th of August? Spell out the Month.

Do you realize there is more than one calendar? Years ago they used the Julian calendar, named after Julius Caesar. In 1582 Pope Gregory XIII changed the calendar for accuracy. However, England and North America didn't start using it until 1752. China didn't start using it until 1949. The new calendar modified leap years and the start of the New Year from March to January. Dates

Citations/Questionnaires/Forms

before 5 January 1752 are often written 26 February 1741/42 indicating the overlap in the calendar.

If the citation isn't about a document but about a conversation say so. Example: Grandma Helene Christine Dahl Patterson told me during a conversation dated 15 January 2002 at her 80th birthday party in St. Paul, MN. If you can verify the information she is giving you please try.

Correspondence is just as easy. An example of how to record a citation for information received in a letter (e-mail):

> Received from Great Aunt Sarah May Johnson, dated 15 January 2002
>
> Scanned and filed under: mydocuments/genealogy/Johnson/SarahMayLetter-15Jan2002.jpg
>
> Original filed at the home of Vickie Chupurdia, Street, City, State, Zip
>
> File located in the filing cabinets.

Hearsay just doesn't cut in with genealogy. When people read your information in the future they want proof, they want documentation. They don't want to just take your word for it. Some will not believe it. It isn't what they remembered or it isn't what Aunt Sarah told them.

There have been several times when I have visited with people and start telling of my findings and they disagree with me. I show them the proof and suddenly they are saying, "Well I'll be. That isn't what I remember at all. My mind must be playing tricks on me."

If you enter your sources in your software program many of them will print as footnotes if you ever decide to print a report or family group sheet or even a book.

Questionnaires and Interviews

Interview the oldest family members as soon as possible. They have memories full of treasures and most elderly people love to talk about their past. They love the attention and the chance to feel needed. Sometimes it might take a bit of coaxing to get them started. It could be that for years nobody wanted to hear them talk about the 'old days'. They may be surprised to find out that somebody is actually interested in what they have to say.

Contributions from older family members will make your family's history come alive. Family history is more than just 'so and so' begat 'so and so'. It's the joys, the sorrows, the struggles and triumphs that turn just a bunch of facts into your family legacy.

Years from now you will be glad you did. You will be able to pass down those treasured stories for generations to come. They will be able to read your Family Tree information, go back in time, and experience the special cherished memories of their ancestors.

When interviewing people be prepared. Develop a questionnaire. It's also a good idea to have something to jar their memory. Maybe you could start your interview by going through old family photo albums or scrapbooks. Often there is something written on the

Citations/Questionnaires/Forms

back to assist you. If not, you have to rely on the interviewee's memory.

Do they have an old trunk that holds a treasure house full of memories? Is grandpa's old military uniform in there or the outfit your mother wore when she was baptized? Is there an old family Bible?

Maybe grandpa had a wood working shop. Sitting there with him might bring back memories of the rocking horse he made for his oldest daughter.

Have your tape recorder and notepad handy. Gather the oral history that may slip away if you wait too long. Don't be too anxious to finish their thoughts for them. Be patient, wait, let them gather their thoughts, let them relive the memory in their minds before they talk.

**See the appendix for questionnaire ideas.

Forms and Charts

The Pedigree Chart is a good overall visual of you and your ancestors. When numbering your Pedigree Chart and Family Group Sheets it is best to use the Ahnentafel (**ah** –nin-*tah*-ful) numbering system. The first person on your first Pedigree Chart is you. You are number 1. Your father is twice your number, so number 2. Your mother is twice your number plus 1, so 3. After the first person, the numbers of the men are always even and the numbers of the women are always odd. Many of the software programs will do this for you.

While the Pedigree Chart is the overview the Family Group Sheet is the details. Each sheet is based on one family listing the husband, wife and all of their children.

It is on this sheet you record the basic information such as birth, place of birth, marriage, death, burial and so on. From the family group sheet you can easily see essential information and also see where you are missing information.

Genetics and DNA

What is DNA?

DNA testing is another form of today's technology that can open up all kinds of information about your family. It is now possible to look inside your DNA and be able to trace the path of your maternal and paternal ancestry back more than 10,000 years!

Your body is made up of around 100 trillion cells. They come with a set of instructions for our bodies called deoxyribonucleic acid; better known as DNA.

Genetics and genealogy have come together and gives us the opportunity to prove family connections. We can prove relationship to an individual and determine our ancestry. Parentage and siblings DNA testing is being used as adoptees and birth families try to locate and reunite.

Your genes carry specific traits that are passed on from ancient ancestor to ancient ancestor. DNA doesn't tell you an exact person's name and how they are related to you. You need to compare your tests to others and find matches. Depending on the closeness of the match it tells you that you share a common ancestor. Depending on how many markers that match it will show you how long ago this common ancestor lived.

DNA Testing

Men and women can test the mtDNA which traces the origins of the maternal line. Both men and women get mtDNA from their mother. It doesn't check any men in your line, only the women.

Mothers pass mtDNA to both their sons and their daughters, but only daughters carry the mtDNA to the next generation. MtDna gives us information but it isn't nearly as good at the Y because it doesn't connect surnames.

MtDNA can determine if two people are related through a maternal line but it's hard to know when the common ancestor lived. MtDNA is often used to track population movements from years ago between continents. For example, you can use MtDNA to test to see if you have American Indian heritage on your maternal line.

Men can test their Y chromosome to trace the origins of their paternal line. This does not check the women in your line, only the men. That's because women don't get a Y-DNA. If you want to trace your paternal line you will need to convince a father, brother, uncle or cousin to have the test done. You need someone with the same Y-DNA as your biological father to trace your paternal lineage.

Y chromosomes are passed virtually unchanged from father to son. That's why genetic genealogists use portions of the Y chromosome to trace paternal DNA. If there was a change in the surname or an adoption Y DNA will show a relationship even if the names are different.

If two men have matching or similar DNA and they have the same surname they probably have a common ancestor.

Y-DNA is the most widely used test for genealogy. There are 12, 25, 37, and 67 marker tests. The more markers you have tested the more precise the results. They range in price from around $60 to $200 depending on what you get. If you order both the Y-DNA and the mtDNA at the same time you could pay up to up to $350. But remember, you get what you pay for. The higher the price for the tests the more accurate and precise the results are.

Brian Sykes' book The Seven Daughters of Eve is a great book to read to follow up on this subject.

Testing is very easy. You send for a kit, swab your cheek, send it in and wait for the results.

DNA is a great tool to use from your genealogical tool belt. Let's say you think there is a connection between two family members. When you combine DNA with all of your other research you might be able to determine for sure if there really is a relationship.

There are several companies that perform the DNA tests for you. Family Tree DNA, Ancestry DNA, Genealogy DNA and more. Just type in DNA testing company in

Genetics and DNA

your browser and you'll get plenty of hits. Please use a reputable company.

These sites also allow you to post your DNA results without giving out personal information so you and others can compare your matches. There are many DNA databases online for you to join. Some are for specific surnames only or surnames in a certain location, by country and so on. It's an option definitely worth exploring.

As of this writing, Family Tree DNA boasts having the largest database of DNA. They have almost 181,000 Y-DNA records, 110,000 mtDNA records, 5,800 surname projects and 95,000 unique surnames. They have a total of 290,924 records.

Sharing Your Family History

Use Your Imagination

There are as many ways to share your family history as your imagination can come up with. It might be something as simple as saving your database to a GEDCOM file and giving it to another family member that is also doing research

However, to get a bit more creative here are some ideas. It is okay to ask for financial contributions or take orders ahead of time for your projects.

1. Cookbook. What kinds of foods did your ancestor prepare? Get Grandma and all of your aunts to contribute recipes to your book along with a family story to go with it. Add some colonial recipes if you have ancestors from that time period.

Sharing Your Family History

2. Have a potluck and everyone has to bring a dish that the ancestors from the Revolutionary War days would have eaten. Then share stories of your ancestors with everyone.

3. If you're into gardening write a little pamphlet about the types of plants your ancestors might have grown. Other family members can contribute their favorite gardening secrets.

4. Create a book. Some of the genealogy software will have book creation functions. There are many websites to guide you. It could be something as simple as a 3 ring binder. It doesn't have to be a bound book.

5. Create a DVD slide show of photographs with your narration.

6. Create a photo collage

7. Create a calendar and give copies to family members. I made a calendar that included family charts, photos, military records and more. Each month can show one branch of

your tree with small blurbs about their history.

8. Do a headstone rubbing, copy it, frame it, and give it to someone.

9. Sew a quilt for someone. You can get copies of photographs printed onto the material, and/or embroider dates.

10. Interview an elderly member of the family and with their permission record it, make it into an MP3 and share it with others.

Kissing Cousins

I'm sure you'd like to share your research with your grandparents, sisters, brothers and cousins. But, who are your cousins?

Have you ever heard someone talk about their 3rd cousin, once removed? What the heck does that mean? How do they get removed?

Well I'll give you a little lesson.

First cousins have the same grandparents that you do. They are the children of your aunts and uncles.

Second cousins have the same great-grandparents that you do but not the same grandparents as you.

Thirds cousins have two great-great-grandparents in common.

So, okay what's the removed stuff? Once removed means its one generation difference. Your Dad's first cousin would be your first cousin, once removed. Twice removed means there are two generations separation. Your grandfather's first cousin would be your first cousin, twice removed.

I know it's a bit confusing. You can find charts to make it easier through a quick online search.

Summary

You now have more than enough knowledge to have great success tracing your family roots.

Enjoy the time you spend with family listening to stories and family lore. These nuggets of information are treasures and thanks to your efforts they will be recorded and passed down generation to generation.

After interviewing family members they often entrusted me with keepsakes and memorabilia that they have been holding onto for years. Most of them are concerned that nobody will care about these artifacts as much as they do. They are worried they will be tossed out or destroyed. Because of my interest they know that I will cherish and care for these items.

The love letters that Grandpa wrote to Grandma while he was in the service (which you can scan and preserve digitally too), the china creamer and sugar bowl your Great Aunt got as a wedding present, or maybe the

Summary

doilies your Grandmother crocheted are wonderful items to possess.

Whether the inheritance given to you is a touching personal story, a long held family secret, a clue to another ancestor, or a treasured china cup, you are now the steward of all this family information. It's an honor to hold these keys to your past. Other family members and friends will look at you with admiration and respect.

Okay, some will look at you with admiration and respect. Some will think you are a nut case for wanting to trudge through cemeteries and sit in court house vaults for hours doing research. But, even these people will love to hear what you have uncovered. It's just that they would never attempt it themselves.

At the next family reunion or gathering you are going to be the hit of the party. You will captivate your audience with stories and facts. Be prepared because when you tell one story there is going to be somebody in the crowd that will share another one. Always have pen and paper or a recorder. Don't lose the moment.

It is a privilege to be the family's scribe and to pass the gift of the family's heritage down to your children, grand children and great grandchildren.

If you get hooked on genealogy one of the things you need to budget for is books. You will find yourself wanting to purchase books on genealogy, restoring photos, American history, Civil War, local and county books and much more. It's endless.

Genealogy research is an adventure. Your family may have migrated following the same route as Lewis and

Clark. Read about it. Learn how the settlers traveled, what motivated them, how it changed their lives and consequently, yours. You will be richer for it.

Genealogy research is being a detective. You have a large puzzle and you are searching for clues to put the pieces together. I will be honest; there have been many times I have gotten tears in my eyes when I have uncovered information or another clue and located a photograph. When you start doing that, you are what they call an '**over the top genealogist**'.

Congratulations! Enjoy you new adventure!

**See appendix for Interview Questionnaire suggestions.

Appendix

Questionnaire for Interviewing

Self

1. Legal name at birth
2. Were you named after someone
3. Nicknames and why
4. Date of Birth
5. Place of Birth
6. Name of hospital or at home
7. Your physical characteristics (height, color of hair, eyes, etc.)
8. Residence now
9. Places you have lived
10. First job
11. Wage history
12. Different careers/occupations
13. Organizations and Clubs
14. Religious affiliations
15. Military service

Appendix

16. Most important achievements
17. Biggest sacrifice ever made
18. Funniest thing ever happened to you
19. What kind of music do you like
20. What kind of movies/TV
21. Book you read
22. Favorite foods
23. Your wisest decision
24. Your biggest regret
25. Who influenced you the most
26. Places traveled
27. Advice to your children/grandchildren
28. Stories of your grandparents/great-grandparents

Growing Up

29. Games you played as a child
30. Favorite toy
31. Did you have an allowance
32. Chores you did as a child
33. Education- where and how much
34. Did you partake in sports
35. Pets
36. Describe holidays
37. Do you have any family heirlooms or treasures
38. Family stories handed down
39. How was childhood home heated
40. Did you have electricity, candles, kerosene lamps
41. How was food preserved, cellar, ice box, refrigerator
42. Did your family have a garden

43. Did your mother can food
44. Did you hunt
45. Type of clothing worn, store bought or handmade
46. Did you travel and how, train, car, air, ship
47. Did you attend church on Sunday
48. Gifts on birthdays and Christmas
49. Any memorable storms or weather, drought, etc.
50. Did you go swimming
51. Most mischievous thing you did
52. Most trouble you ever got in

Spouse

53. Spouse's full maiden name
54. Date of Birth
55. Place of Birth
56. Name of hospital or at home
57. Education
58. First job
59. Wage history
60. Different careers/occupations
61. Organizations and Clubs
62. Religious affiliations
63. Military service
64. Date of Death
65. Place of Death
66. Place of Burial
67. Occupation

Married Life

68. Date of marriage

Appendix

69. Description of proposal
70. How/where you met
71. Place of marriage
72. Church name or courthouse
73. What you wore
74. Age of both at marriage
75. First house
76. First car
77. Hardships faced
78. Memorable stories
79. Favorite activities together

Children

80. Full names of children
81. Dates of Births
82. Places of Births
83. Dates of Deaths
84. Places of Deaths
85. Places of Burials
86. Spouses full names
87. Children full names
88. Residence
89. Occupations

Parents

90. Mother's full maiden name
91. Nicknames and why
92. Date of Birth
93. Place of Birth
94. Name of hospital or at home

95. Date of Death
96. Place of Death
97. Place of Burial
98. Occupation
99. Organizations and Clubs
100. Religious affiliation
101. Father's full name
102. Nicknames and why
103. Date of Birth
104. Place of Birth
105. Name of hospital or at home
106. Date of Death
107. Place of Death
108. Place of Burial
109. Occupations
110. Organizations and Clubs
111. Religious affiliation
112. How/when did they meet
113. How did he propose
114. Date of marriage
115. Place of marriage
116. Church name or courthouse
117. Special character traits of parents
118. Military service

Siblings

119. Name of siblings
120. Nicknames and why
121. Date of Births
122. Places of Births
123. Date of Deaths
124. Places of Death

Appendix

125. Places of Burial
126. Spouses names
127. Date of marriages
128. Childhood memories of siblings

Grandparents

129. Maternal parent's names
130. Dates of Birth
131. Places of Birth
132. Dates of Deaths
133. Places of Deaths
134. Places of Burial
135. Occupations
136. Organizations and Clubs
137. Religious affiliation
138. Places lived
139. Paternal parent's names
140. Dates of Births
141. Places of Births
142. Dates of Deaths
143. Places of Deaths
144. Places of Burial
145. Occupations
146. Organizations and Clubs
147. Religious affiliation
148. Places lived

About the Author – Vintage Vickie

www.VintageVickie.com

Vickie Chupurdia lives in northeastern Minnesota. She has been doing extensive genealogy research and family histories for the past 30 years. She has traveled the world for the past 20 years as a software consultant experiencing other cultures and customs.

Vickie has won awards for her writing and plans on continuing this enterprise. She is available for 'missing heir' research, seminars, workshops and speaking engagements, and has taught genealogy at the collegiate level.

She is a member of:

- APG - Association of Professional Genealogists
- APH - Association of Personal Historians

Appendix

- ISFHWE – International Society of Family History Writers and Editors
- NGS – National Genealogical Society
- MHS - Minnesota Historical Society
- MGS - Minnesota Genealogical Society
- TPGS - Twin Ports Genealogical Society
- DAR – Daughter's of the American Revolution
- PWA – Professional Writers Alliance
- ITWPA - International Travel Writers & Photographers Alliance
- AWAI – American Writers & Artists, Inc.

Made in the USA
Charleston, SC
21 September 2014